GENERAL HEADQUARTERS
UNITED STATES ARMY FORCES, PACIFIC
MILITARY INTELLIGENCE SECTION, GENERAL STAFF

HISTORY OF
TECHNICAL INTELLIGENCE

SOUTHWEST AND WESTERN PACIFIC AREAS

1942 — 1945

VOLUME I

U.S. ARMY TECHNICAL INTELLIGENCE CENTER

Published by Books Express Publishing
Copyright © Books Express, 2011
ISBN 978-1-780392-09-7

Books Express publications are available from all good retail and online booksellers. For
publishing proposals and direct ordering please contact us at: info@books-express.com

The 5250th Technical Intelligence Company: Technical Intelligence in

the Southwest and Western Pacific Areas, 1942-1945.

The outbreak of war in December 1941 found the United States Army
generally unprepared, especially in the field of technical intelligence.
Enemy equipment captured in the Southwest Pacific Area (SWPA) was, until
1942, only given brief examination by Ordnance or Chemical Warfare Service
officers before forwarding to the Australian Army General Staff, Intelligence (10) for examination and testing.

Training Circular No. 81, issued in November 1942, established pro-
ceedures for the evacuation of captured materiel, but responsibility for
analysis remained with the Theater staff officers of the services and, to
a large extent, with the Australian Army. The situation began to improve
in late December 1942, when five Ordnance officers and ten enlisted
personnel, all trained in technical intelligence at Aberdeen Proving
Ground, Maryland, and Washington, D.C., arrived at Headquarters, US Army
Service of Supply (USASOS), Base 3, Brisbane, Australia. On 30 December,
Major Alan C. Johnston, the ranking officer, was tasked to organize an
Ordnance Technical Intelligence Unit for the Theater. The unit was to be
under the control of the Chief Ordnance Officer, USASOS, in accordance
with policies established by the Assistant Chief of Staff, G-2 (ACofS,G-2),
USASOS. The original organization called for an Administrative Section,
an Ordnance Analysis Section, and several Technical Intelligence Field
Teams. The latter were designed to operate from an advance base or with
a regular combat unit. The Field Teams usually consisted of one officer
and one or more enlisted personnel, and had the mission of collecting
enemy equipment and sending it back to the Ordnance Analysis Section for
examination and evaluation. Assignments were flexible and personnel were
often used interchangeably in the different sections.

Responsibility for technical intelligence was turned over to the
US Army Forces Far East (USAFFE) in February 1943, and Major Johnston
was appointed USAFFE Technical Intelligence Officer, under the direct
control of the Chief Ordnance Officer, USAFFE. Except for an enlisted
assistant, all other Ordnance technical intelligence personnel were
carried under the T/O's of the Ordnance Office, USASOS, and the various
USASOS Base Sections.

Until February 1943, Chemical Warfare Service staff officers made
preliminary examinations of captured chemical equipment and munitions,
but evacuation and technical analysis remained the responsibility of
the Australian Army. With the formation of USAFFE in February, a
Chemical Warfare Intelligence Section was formed from locally available
personnel. The Section originally consisted of two officers and one
enlisted man, designated the Chemical Intelligence Section, USASOS, and
three field teams of one officer and one enlisted each.

On 27 May 1943, Headquarters USAFFE directed the Commanding General,
USASOS, to establish a salvage depot for captured enemy equipment near

the Australian depot at Base Section 3. Although the Ordnance and
Chemical Warfare Service Analysis Sections were still separate from
the salvage depot, its establishment was the first step toward a coordinated technical intelligence effort. Coordination for the analysis
of equipment captured by US and Australian forces after it reached the
joint salvage depot area was the responsibility of the newly established Joint Allied Captured Enemy Equipment Board. During this period
both Ordnance and Chemical Warfare Service field teams operated with
Allied forces in New Guinea.

On 29 September 1943, all Ordnance personnel were transferred
from USAFFE to USASOS control. Headquarters USASOS began planning
for the establishment of a Technical Intelligence Depot with sections
from all services except Signal and Engineer. Before the plans could
be implemented, a 22 December 1943 USAFFE directive, "Responsibility
of Technical Intelligence," delegated the responsibility for ground
technical intelligence to the CG, USASOS, and directed him to establish
a Technical Intelligence Depot along slightly different lines.

After study of the directive, the ACofS, G-2, USASOS, recommended
the formation of a Technical Intelligence Composite Company utilizing
personnel from all technical services except Transportation. The
company would operate under defined T/O's and T/E's and would provide
for greater centralization and flexibility of the technical intelligence
effort. The recommendations were forwarded to the CG, USAFFE, on 7
December 1943, and were approved. General Orders No. 2, Headquarters
USASOS, dated 3 January 1944, announced the organization of the 5250th
Technical Intelligence Composite Company, Separate (Provisional), under
the T/O's submitted in the 7 December recommendations. Personnel were
to be carried on Detached Service from their source units, and each
service section was to operate under the general supervision of the
chief of the service concerned. The problem of provisional organization was that personnel detailed to the 5250th were still carried
on the rosters of their source units, making promotion difficult. The
formation of the 5250th as other than a provisional unit was un-
favorably considered by USAFFE on 10 January. The ACofS, G-2, USASOS,
directed the chiefs of all six services to furnish qualified personnel for the 5250th on 20 January 1944, and all transfers were made
by February 1944.

The 5250th was organized with a Coordination and Administration
Section, and a Technical Section for each of the represented services.
Each Technical Section was to be composed of a Laboratory Element and
several Enemy Equipment Intelligence Teams. However, on the Ordnance,
Signal, and Quartermaster Sections operated analysis laboratories at
this time. Chemical analysis was done at either the 42d Chemical or
the Victoria Munitions Supply laboratories. Engineer and Medical Services
did not have teams in the field until the Hollandia operation in April
1944. General supervision over the 5250th was furnished by the ACofS,
G-2, USASOS. Major Johnston continued as Acting Commanding Officer, having
no orders appointing him to command as yet. He also served in the Office
of the ACofS, G-2, USASOS, as Technical Intelligence Coordinator.

In December 1943, just prior to the organization of the 5250th Technical Intelligence Company, the G-2, USAFFE, had been requested to ask Sixth Army to permit a Combined Technical Intelligence Field Unit (Ordnance and Chemical Warfare Services) to participate in the Cape Gloucester operation. The Combined Field Team was authorized but Sixth Army would not allow it forward of Finschhafen, although a three-man Ordnance Team did get to Saidor from January to March 1944. For the Admiralty Islands operation (29 February - 18 May 1944), Ordnance and Chemical Warfare Service Technical Intelligence Field Teams were attached to the Counterintelligence Corps (CIC) Teams supporting the 1st Cavalry Division. The CIC officer was in charge of each of the combined teams, which also included personnel from the Naval Mobile Explosives Investigation Unit. The first technical intelligence personnel landed on 6 March (D+6). This was the first campaign in which members of more than one technical service's operations were coordinated and it proved that a larger area could be covered in less time using this method.

Planning began for the Hollandia operation. Four officers from the Military Intelligence Training Center at Camp Ritchie, Maryland, and one officer and 14 enlisted personnel from the 234th Quartermaster Salvage Collecting Company arrived at the Finschhafen Depot. Both separate service and combined teams, and a composite unit were to be formed for the operation. Separate Ordnance and Chemical Warfare Service Technical Intelligence Teams supported the 41st Infantry Division, while a combination of Chemical Warfare Service and Naval Mobile Explosives Investigation Unit Teams were attached to the CIC Team in support of the ACofS, G-2, 24th Infantry Division. Technical Intelligence Composite Unit #1 was formed between 13 and 23 April and consisted of nine officers and three enlisted men representing the six technical services. Unit #1 landed on 30 April (D+8) and went into operation. Engineer Field Team #3, the first Engineer Team to operate in the field, joined the Composite Unit for a short time, then departed for operations on Biak Island.

Letter, GSB 323.3, HQ USASOS, dated 25 March 1944, and Letter, FEGB, 386.3, HQ USAFFE, dated 28 March 1944, authorized the establishment of a US Army Technical Intelligence Depot at Finschhafen effective 20 April 1944. During July and August the various laboratory analysis sections moved from Brisbane to Finschhafen, thus reducing the distance between collectors (field teams) and evaluators (laboratories). The combining of the Laboratory Analysis Sections and the Receiving-Shipping Section at both Finschhafen and at the tempory Composite Unit #1 field deport at Hollandia resulted in more efficient operations.

Various Field Teams participated in the Biak Island (27 May - 20 August 1944) and Sansapor (30 July - 31 August 1944) operations. In July, one officer was placed on detached service from the 5250th, and became the Technical Intelligence Coordinator with Headquarters, Sixth Army-a move which greatly enhanced the technical intelligence coordination effort. On 25 August, Major Eugene H. Manley, CE, was officially appointed as Commanding Officer, 5250th Technical Intelligence Composite Company, Separate (Provisional), and as the Technical Intelligence Coordinator to the ACofS, G-2, USASOS. Major Johnston, the former CO, assumed command of the Ordnance Technical Intelligence Section for the forthcoming Philippine Islands operation. By 31 August 1944, the 5250th consisted of 16 officers and 25 enlisted personnel from the War Department and 30 officers and 30 enlisted personnel from Theater technical service units.

Although technical intelligence units continued to support the island hopping operations, emphasis was placed on preparations for the Philippine Islands operations. Plans for the Leyte phase envisioned three composite technical intelligence units - Technical Intelligence Unit #1 (Ordnance, Signal and Engineer) with the 24th Infantry Division; Unit #2 (all six technical services) with the 1st Cavalry Division; and Unit #3 (all six technical services) with the Army Service Command and further detached to Headquarters, Base K, at Tacloban, Leyte. Unit #1 was attached with the CIC Team under the ACofS, G-2, 24th Infantry Division, and landed with the second wave. After eight days of operations, Unit #1 returned to the Technical Intelligence Depot at Finschhafen. The Officer-in-Charge of Unit #2 also served as the Technical Intelligence Coordinator to Sixth Army. On 1 November, Unit #2 also returned to the Finschhafen Depot. Unit #3 landed on 21 October (D+1) and acted as a forward provisional depot for Units #1 and 2 until their return to Finschhafen.

In November, after the return of the Technical Intelligence Composite Units to Finschaffen, another reorganization of the 5250th took place. Personnel from Units #1-3 were used as nuclei for the formation of Units #4-7 for the Luzon Campaign. On 14 November, the Technical Intelligence Coordinator and a reorganized Unit #1 were attached to Headquarters, Eighth Army for the remainder of the Leyte operation. In December, Field Units #1-7 moved out to join their combat units for the Luzon operation. Initially, a Technical Intelligence Composite Unit was attached to each division under supervision of the division G-2. Experience soon demonstrated that greater flexibility could be obtained by assigning units to corps, where they functioned under the corps G-2 and technical service staff officers, and from which they could be assigned to the areas of most need. In addition, one unit was designated as Sixth Army Headquarters Unit. The limited quantities of captured medical and quartermaster equipment made it unnecessary to assign technical personnel from these branches any lower than corps level. One Ordnance technican was detailed to special duty with the Special Intelligence Section, Sixth Army, to collect and repair weapons and equipment for issue to Filipino guerrilla forces. A special team, designated the JAPLAT Team, was formed to collect data from Japanese equipment nameplates to satisfy a requirement from the Military Intelligence Division in Washington.

Field Units #1-7 took part in the initial Luzon operations, with Unit #3 again functioning as the forward provisional depot, first at San Jacinto and then at Angeles. By March, Field Units #1, 2, 3, 6, and 7 had been relieved of field duties and had returned to the Depot. Field Units #4, 5, 8, and 9 (the latter having been formed during the operation) remained on field duty with their combat units.

With the opening of the Luzon Campaign, steps were taken to close down the US Army Technical Intelligence Depot at Finschhafen and to move it, except for a rear-echelon force, to Manila when that city should be captured. Operations at Finschhafen ceased 28 February 1945, and the move began on 12 March. After the capture of Manila, the new US Army Technical Intelligece Depot was established there on 26 March, with eight officers and 38 enlisted personnel. The 5250th had 68 officers and 139 enlisted personnel in February, with nine field units attached to Sixth Army (36 officers and 60 enlisted), and three field units attached to Eighth Army (16 officers and 27 enlisted), but by March had grown to 90 officers and 185 enlisted personnel with a total of 72 field teams.

Headquarters Eighth Army Circular #138, dated 10 May 1945, directed that the the technical intelligence teams in its area of operations would come under the operational, administrative, and technical control of the respective technical service chiefs and would coordinate with the G-2 of the unit tho which they were attached. Field Unit #1, once again re-organized, was split into various teams--referred to by the prefix Victor and a number--for mopping-up operations in the southern Philippines. Most of the Victor teams had completed their missions by June 1945 and had re-turned to the Depot. Planning was begun for Operations Olympic and Coronet--the invasion of Japan. Headquarters AFPAC tasked AFWESPAC and Sixth Army to provide 52 officers and 97 enlisted men divided into a "field depot", five "A" and five "B" units. The Field Depot Unit would consist of two officers and seven enlisted, and would include Ordnance, Quartermaster, and JAPLAT teams. The type "A" field units would consist of six officers and ten enlisted, and would include teams from all six technical services plus a JAPLAT team. The type "B" field units would consist of four officers and eight enlisted, composed of Ordnance, Signal, Engineer, Chemical, and JAPLAT teams. At this time, the 5250th was augmented by the arrival of HHD, 98th Quartermaster Battalion.

Japan's surrender put an end to the invasion planning, but the 5250th was alerted to move the field units to Japan on 23 August. The 5250th was further strengthened with the arrival of 38 officers and 58 enlisted personnel. The "A" units, designated Field Teams #1-5, the "B" units, designated as Field Teams #51-55, and the depot, designated Field Depot Unit #71, departed Manila for Japan during late August and early September 1945. The original organization was modified slightly and the total strength of these units was 53 officers and 100 enlisted. The Field Units were assigned to the subordinate corps of the Sixth and Eighth Armies and the Field Depot Unit was attached to Sixth Army Headquarters.

GHQ, AFPAC General Orders #337 and 369, dated 20 and 30 November 1945, reassigned the 5250thc to the direct control of GHQ, AFPAC. GO #337 established the 5250th Technical Intelligence Company as a Theater overhead installation with an authorized strength of 90 officers and 261 enlisted personnel. GO #369 dissolved the 5250th Technical Intelligence Composite Company, (Separate) Provisional. LTC Manley remained as the Commanding Officer and LTC David S. Tait became the Technical Intelligence Coordinator.

The 5250th was also assigned responsibility for the United States Army Technical Intelligence Center, which had been established under the G-2, GHQ, Supreme Commander Allied Powers (SCAP). The Technical Intelligence Depot began to shut down operations in October, the personnel departed Manila between 6 and 9 November, and the unit closed in Tokyo on 20 November 1945.

Upon arrival in Japan, the 5250th personnel were assigned to Special Troops, GHQ, SCAP, although they worked under the control of the ACofS, G-2, GHQ, SCAP. They worked through the War Department Technical Intelligence Targeting Section (WDIT), which was headed by COL Walter S. Wood. The WDIT decided what captured enemy equipment and which enemy installations would be exploited under the provisions of General Orders #9 and 15, 2 October and 9 November 1945. LTC Tait became the head of the Technical Intelligence Section for WDIT operations. The 5250th examined a number of installations and a large amount of Japanese industrial and military equipment.

The end of hostilities saw the beginning of the demise of the 5250th and of the decline of technical intelligence in the United States Army. Technical intelligence organizations were revived during the Korean and Vietnam conflicts and were based, in large part, on the lessons learned from the 5250th, but technical intelligence remained almost dormant between actual hostilities--an extremely valuable but neglected field of intelligence.

HEADQUARTERS
5250th TECHNICAL INTELLIGENCE COMPANY

VOLUME I

Tokyo, Japan
7 December 1945

VOLUME II

Inclosures 1 - 34 inclusive

EUGENE H. MANLEY
Lt Colonel   GSC
Commanding

4740

U.S. Army Technical Intelligence
Center, Tokyo

HISTORY OF TECHNICAL INTELLIGENCE

IN THE

SOUTHWEST AND WESTERN PACIFIC AREAS

1942 -- 1946

INTRODUCTION

When the United States was plunged into a Far Eastern war
with Japan by the bombing of Pearl Harbor on 7 December 1941,
we came face to face with the fact that we knew little or nothing about that Island empire. What had Japan in the way of an
Army and Navy? What about their Marianas outposts and the other
Jap mandated islands? How and with what weapons would the Japanese fight?

Many of these questions in the early phases of the war were
unanswered. We had a war on our hands yet we were uncertain of
the enemy's capabilities. Our Technical Intelligence was practically non-existent -- , and we almost lost the war as a result.
We found the enemy much more potent than most strategists had
expected, and we paid for underestimating his strength with a
series of strategic withdrawals to the south. We lost important
bases for a counter offensive -- the Philippines, Hong Kong,
Singapore, Java, Borneo, the entire group of islands to the
north of New Guinea, even the northern portion of New Guinea
itself.

With only two American and two Australian divisions between them and a completion of the conquest of the whole Western Pacific, the Japs were finally stopped on the Kokoda Trail
(Map, Incl 1) in their drive toward the Allied base at Port
Moresby.

The comeback looked long and hard. Over three thousand
miles of ocean with thousands of Jap-garrisoned islands lay
between us and Tokyo. We now knew the enemy's capabilities
and how absolutely his whole home economy had been geared to
total war, but an army in retreat learns little of the enemy's
materiel, equipment and weapons, except their terrific effect.

These were among the major objectives of the Allies: to
know what weapons the enemy had so that we could devise

1

countermeasures and countertactics of our own; to exploit important discoveries for our own benefit; to win the technological race.

In the earliest months of the war the United States had a mere handful of Technical Intelligence men in the Pacific Theater, dependent for training upon the Australian Army. Then Technical Intelligence was taken over by the Ordnance and Chemical Warfare Service sections of the United States Army Forces Far East (USAFFE) under the supervision of their respective service chiefs. Their operations, beginning in a small way, culminated 3 January 1944 in the formation of a coordinated organization of the six major services, the 5250th Technical Intelligence Composite Company, Separate (Provisional). The 470 technical experts administered through this company kept the Allied Forces informed of Japanese progress in arms, ammunition and equipment. They were the eyes and the ears of the army in the battle of the Pacific.

As differentiated from the enemy in Europe, the Japanese fought, in many cases, on a shoestring; their tenuous supply lines, reaching to the various island groups, were generally severed before the Allied troops went into operation and backlogs of enemy supplies were consequently well depleted; surrender en masse, such as occurred in Europe, with the accompanying seizure of large stores of enemy supplies, was unknown in the war with Japan until the summer of 1945 -- when the war was over. The capture, then, of any considerable quantity of Japanese equipment was a matter of great Intelligence importance.

The following pages trace the development and operations of Technical Intelligence from New Guinea to the Philippines to the occupation of Japan. This is the history of the pioneers of Technical Intelligence in the Pacific, an integral, vital -- and now we know -- indispensable part of the history of the United States Army.

C H A P T E R I

TECHNICAL INTELLIGENCE BY ORDNANCE AND CHEMICAL WARFARE SERVICE

December 1942 -- January 1944

From the opening of the Pacific War until November 1942, there was little Technical Intelligence activity in the Southwest Pacific Area (SWPA). A few small arms and some ammunition plus a few items of Chemical Warfare equipment were turned into the Ordnance and Chemical Warfare officers for examination and then forwarded by both American and Australian forces to the Australian Army for examin- ation, test and report. No organized attempt had been made, how- ever, to have Technical Intelligence carried into the field by a team of men skilled in collecting and analyzing captured enemy equipment.

Technical Intelligence in Accordance with Training Circular No. 81

In November 1942, Training Circular No. 81 established a more closely knit control for processing captured enemy equipment of In- telligence value. The flow of materiel was from combat troops (there were, as yet, no Technical Intelligence teams) to service troops in the combat zone, to the theater special staff officer of the appro- priate service, to the Chief of the appropriate service in the United States. Flow of informational reports was through channels from the combat troops to the S-2 or G-2, to the Assistant Chief of Staff, G-2, (AC of S) to the War Department, as well as interchangeably with the service troops handling the materiel.

Combat personnel capturing equipment of new design sent it rearward through normal recovery channels together with accessories, ammunition, and pertinent information, each service handling its own equipment. Simultaneously, a report was rendered through channels.

Maintenance and supply service personnel delivered captured equipment, with no maintenance other than the application of pre- servatives, direct to the Theater special staff officer of the same arm or service or to his designated establishment (such as a base shop or depot). Report was made at the same time to the G-2 of their command. Both combat and maintenance personnel recovering a new type of materiel of a class supplied by another service delivered it to the nearest organization of the appropriate service.

Theater staff officers were responsible for preliminary expert analysis as to the characteristics of the materiel. Based upon this, they made preliminary deductions as to the state of enemy resources for war, as evidenced by the materiel, and published preliminary operator's and maintenance manuals, with instructions on local modifications that could be made so that the captured equipment could be used by United Nations troops in the field. These reports, together with the captured materiel (half of the captured materiel went to the Australians, half to the United States) were then transmitted to the chief of the arm or service concerned in the United States. Complete reports were also made by the Theater staff officers to the G-2 of the Theater staff, and necessary arrangements were made when possible to exploit the enemy materiel when captured in large quantities.

The chief of each supply arm or service in the Zone of the Interior made final analysis and deductions and prepared final operator's and maintenance manuals and visual training aids.

The Theater G-2, under the provisions of this circular, it will be noted, merely transmitted information on the equipment and had no responsibility in its processing.

Ordinance Technical Intelligence: Dec 1942 -- Jan 1944.

As the battle for Buna and Gona, New Guinea, was drawing to a close in December 1942, a group of five Ordnance officers and ten enlisted men was preparing to leave the United States for the Southwest Pacific Area. These men were specialists in ammunition, small arms, artillery, fire control equipment, and tracked and wheeled vehicles. Previous to their departure they had been given an intensive indoctrination in Ordnance Technical Intelligence at Aberdeen Proving Ground, Maryland, and at Washington, D. C.

HISTORY OF TECHNICAL INTELLIGENCE

On arrival at Headquarters, United States Army Service of Supply (USASOS), Base 3, Brisbane, Australia, on 30 December 1942, Major Alan C. Johnston, ranking officer, was placed in charge of the group to set up an Ordnance Technical Intelligence organization for the Theater. The program was to operate under the technical control of the Chief Ordnance Officer, USASOS, in accordance with general policies established by the Assistant Chief of Staff, G-2, of that headquarters.

The detachment was broken down into three sections: The Administrative Section, besides being responsible for the general supervision of Ordnance Intelligence activities, issued reports, maintained liaison with United States and Australian Technical Intelligence organizations in other theaters, collected new data issued in the Pacific Theater on Japanese Ordnance materiel, and forwarded this information to the Chief of Ordnance, Washington, D. C. (Technical Intelligence personnel in the Southwest Pacific Area and the Western Pacific assigned to Headquarters Administration throughout the war are shown in Incl 2).

The second section consisted of Technical Intelligence Field Teams composed of an officer and one or more enlisted men, who operated from an advance base or with a task force, division or corps. Their duties were to collect, identify, prepare preliminary reports on new items, and ship captured Japanese materiel to the Ordnance Analysis Section. (Technical Intelligence personnel in the SWPA and Western Pacific Area (WESPAC) assigned to field teams and the operations in which they participated are shown in Incl 3).

The third was the Ordnance Analysis Section, located at Brisbane, Australia, which received materiel from field teams, analyzed and prepared reports on new items, prepared and shipped Japanese Ordnance materiel to United States troops in the Theater for training and to the United States for Technical investigation and training, and maintained liaison with Technical investigation and training, and maintained liaison with Technical Intelligence organizations in the vicinity (such as the Allied Translator and Interpreter Section (ATIS) of General Headquarters, (GHQ) SWPA, with General Staff, Intelligence, (10) of the Australian Army at Australian Land Headquarters and with the Master General of Ordnance, in Melbourne). (Personnel assigned to analysis work in the Technical Intelligence Depots are shown in Incl 4.)

HISTORY OF TECHNICAL INTELLIGENCE

This first detachment of Technical Intelligence personnel assigned to the Pacific -- all Ordnance -- were allocated as designated below:

Headquarters Section

Maj Alan C. Johnston, O.I.C.   S/Sgt Paul F. Quick, Chf Clk
Capt Donald F. Madigan, Asst   Cpl Albert Beveridge, Clk

Ordnance Technical Intelligence Team

1st Lt Truman B. Pash   T/4 Raymond J. Levy
1st Lt Ernest V. Camer   T/4 John B. Winn
T/Sgt Glenn E. Peters

Ordnance Analysis Section

Lt Eugene D. White   T/3 John L. Lischalk
T/Sgt George W. Bruner   Sgt Clement J. Kusnierek
S/Sgt Roethell W. Loveless   Cpl Harry R. O'Meara

There was considerable flexibility in these assignments and they were often used interchangeably, i.e., headquarters and analysis section personnel went into the field and vice versa. As it turned out, Capt Madigan, S/Sgt Loveless and Sgt Kusnierek were with Headquarters USASOS till February 1943 when they were transferred to the analysis section at Brisbane. From January until July, when part of the personnel was pulled for field work, the Ordnance analysis section reported in great detail on practically all of the materiel that was captured. They issued 26 complete technical reports -- one report on the 75mm AA gun, over 50 pages long, and contained 30 photographs.

Technical Intelligence personnel received training and information from the Australian Army in the early days, which was quite valuable. As an example, Capt Madigan and two enlisted men spent 19 days in Melbourne in January 1943, at the Office of the Master General of Ordnance in Wesley College, looking over their complete collection of Japanese Ordnance, taking the weapons apart, studying and analyzing them.

Though Technical Intelligence was never actually under the Australian Army for administration, except in the same capacity as other United States forces were attached for early operations, the alliance and cooperation was close and was of great benefit to both armies.

HISTORY OF TECHNICAL INTELLIGENCE

Later, in February 1943, when Technical Intelligence was turned over to United States Army Forces Far East (USAFFE), Major Johnston was appointed Technical Intelligence officer, operating under the direct control of the Chief Ordnance Officer, USAFFE. The only personnel assigned to Headquarters USAFFE at that time were Major Johnston and S/Sgt Quick. All other Ordnance Technical Intelligence personnel were carried on the T/O of the Ordnance Office, USASOS, and various Base Sections.

Capt Madigen, at that time operating out of Base "B", Oro Bay, New Guinea, (Map Incl 1) took charge of all field teams; he also assumed responsibility for investigating the Japanese Ordnance material held by the Master General of Ordnance, Australian Army; and from 6 March to 11 July 1943 went on temporary duty with the 42d Chemical Laboratory Company to investigate Japanese explosives and ammunitions.

Chemical Warfare Service: Dec 1942 -- Jan 1944

Whereas Ordnance Technical Intelligence personnel had been sent directly to the Pacific from the United States, the Chemical Warfare Intelligence Section was formed locally.

Throughout 1942, new types of captured enemy equipment were sent to the Chemical Warfare Service Intelligence Officer, Headquarters, New Guinea Forces, Australia, who made the preliminary examination and determined its operational significance. It was then sent to Land Headquarters, Australian Army, Melbourne, (later, Advance Land Headquarters, Brisbane) for Technical Intelligence. Land Headquarters then issued the equipment to the appropriate arm or service for complete technical analysis and report. Chemical Warfare munitions were sent to either 42d Chemical Laboratory or the Victoria Munitions Supply Laboratory, Marybyrnong, Victoria, Australia. The entire channel of evacuation was Australian.

This was improved somewhat in January 1943, when arrangements were made for United States Chemical Warfare Intelligence Officers to be notified of materiel sent back from the forward area by United States forces so that they could work with Land Headquarters, Australian Army, on the disposition of that materiel.

There was, however, no established Chemical Warfare Intelligence organization. The work was carried on as one of the functions of the chemical laboratories under the supervision of the Technical Intelligence officer of the Chemical Warfare Section, Headquarters, USASOS. Their analysis consisted merely of examining and reporting on Japanese chemical materiel.

It became apparent that in addition to the laboratory analysis, an organization was needed which could collect equipment and study Japanese tactics, methods and preparations for chemical warfare. In February 1943, when USAFFE was activated, a Chemical Warfare Section was set up in that Headquarters with an Intelligence officer detailed to formulate plans for more comprehensive Intelligence organization.

At this time there were two officers and one enlisted man in the Chemical Intelligence Section, Headquarters, USASOS: Major John A. Riddick, 1st Lt William J. Roberts, and S/Sgt Vernon G. Phipps. To these was added another officer, 2d Lt James D. Masson, responsible for documents research and publications.

In addition, three officers and three enlisted men were assigned to three field Chemical Warfare Intelligence teams working under the direction of Headquarters USAFFE in the forward areas. Assignments were as follows:

CWS Intelligence Team No. 1

2d Lt William J. Barry   Pfc Paul R. Going

CWS Intelligence Team No. 2

2d Lt Robert W. Bond   Pfc John P. Garner

CWS Intelligence Team No. 3

2d Lt Donald B. Henry   Cpl Leon C. Schier

On 27 May 1943 the Commanding General, USASOS, was directed by par 5, Circular No. 31, Headquarters USAFFE (Incl 5) to "establish at Base Section 3 a salvage depot for captured enemy equipment, conveniently located in relation to the captured enemy equipment depot of the Australian Army now located in Base Section 3". The Ordnance and Chemical Warfare Service analysis sections were still separate from the depot, which was used only for shipping and receiving equipment; and still there was no Technical Intelligence by Engineers, Medical Corps, Quartermaster or Signal Corps; nevertheless, it was the first step toward coordination. 1st Lt Orrie P. Sell, Jr., QMC, was placed in charge of the depot.

HISTORY OF TECHNICAL INTELLIGENCE

At the same time, Technical Intelligence of the United States and Australia was more closely coordinated through the activation of the Joint Allied Captured Enemy Equipment Board which replaced Land Headquarters in determining the final disposition of captured equipment. All materiel received at both the United States and Australian depots was checked by the Allied Enemy Equipment Board for disposition. The Board, consisting of two members from the United States, two from the Australian forces, and one from Allied Naval Forces, made disposition of materiel based on Technical training needs. This permitted both forces to obtain items which might not otherwise be available. Major Johnston was appointed as a member of this board in June 1943 and again, with Lt Sell, in December 1943.

During the period 16 June to 8 September 1943, Lt Barry and Pfc Going of C/S Intelligence Team No. 1 were sent on temporary duty to United States Advance Base, Port Moresby, New Guinea (Map Incl 1). Their mission was to establish liaison with Technical Intelligence units from United States Army Ordnance, Fifth Air Force, Naval Intelligence, the Royal Australian Air Force, and Headquarters New Guinea Forces. They were to clarify the channels through which enemy materiel and Intelligence reports and equipment would go, and to provide that such channels were functioning properly. At the same time, the team was to be prepared to proceed to any area to investigate matters of interest to Chemical Warfare.

Buna -- Gona -- Sananando: 9 Dec 1942 -- 22 Jan 1943

The Buna -- Gona -- Sananando, New Guinea (Map, Incl 1) operations were conducted jointly by Australian forces and by I Corps, with the 32d Division bearing the brunt of the fighting.

Ordnance Technical Intelligence which had just arrived in the Theater in December had a team in the field by 18 January. Lt Bishop, Lt Cameron, and four enlisted men were sent to Port Moresby to stage for two weeks for Buna -- Gona. During the next six months they covered this entire area and shipped back much valuable Ordnance equipment to Brisbane for analysis.

In June, Lt Bishop and Sgt Peterson returned to Brisbane to relieve Capt Madigan and S/Sgt Loveless in the analysis section, and Capt Madigan left immediately to go north to join the field detail in Guinea.

HISTORY OF TECHNICAL INTELLIGENCE

Nassau Bay: 30 Jun 1943

On 30 June 1943 the McKechnie Force, composed of elements of the 41st Infantry Division attached to the 5th Australian Division, landed at Nassau Bay (Map, Incl 1) and quickly mopped up the small enemy garrison there. An Ordnance T. I. Team consisting of Capt Madigan, officer in charge, Lt Cameron, T/4 Winn, and T/4 Levy, came up from the Buna -- Gona area in early July so that they might be on hand before the equipment and material could be destroyed or souvenired by United States troops. Lt Cameron, Levy and Winn left during August for Brisbane and Capt Madigan was joined a week later by S/Sgt Loveless and Cpl O'Meara from the Ordnance Analysis Section. This put all new men in the field, furnishing a turnover of personnel for combat duty. As the offensive followed up the coast, the newly formed Ordnance T. I. Team continued operations with the combat troops.

CWS Intelligence Team No. 3, Lt Henry and Cpl Schier, covered the Nassau Bay operation for CWS. Air transportation from Brisbane was obtained by the team on 25 June to Port Moresby, thence across the Owen Stanley Range to Dobodura, near Oro Bay (Map Incl 1).

Here the team was attached to the Chemical Section, Headquarters 41st Infantry Division, and spent two weeks going through the old battlegrounds in the Buna -- Gona area where they contacted the men who had taken part in the action and who were at this time established in defensive positions along the beach (the operation had "closed" 22 January...). The team was then attached to the McKechnie Force and sailed 12 July for Morobe and later on up to Nassau Bay, (Map Incl 1).

On 22 July, their mission completed, Cpl Schier was dispatched with the Chemical Warfare captured equipment to the Chemical Officer, 41st Infantry Division, and Lt Henry left 28 July for Oro Bay, reporting to Headquarters 41st Infantry Division and from there flew to Brisbane.

Lae -- Salamaua: 4 Sep 1943 -- 16 Sep 1943

On 4 September 1943 under cover of heavy air and naval bombardment, a large Australian force landed and established beachheads fifteen miles northeast of Lae, cutting the enemy's line of communications to Finschhafen and the north coast of New Guinea, (Map Incl 1). On the following day, preceded by heavy bombing and the United States strafing, 503d Parachute Infantry Regiment parachuted and captured the airfield at Nadzab (a few miles northwest of Lae). Airborne troops were quickly moved in, and following a rapid advance by both forces, Lae fell to the Allied on 16 September 1943.

Meanwhile, Salamaua (Map Incl 1) had fallen on 11 September and the remnants of four Japanese divisions, half-starved and malaria ridden, were pursued back east along the coast toward Morobe, bitterly contesting every Allied gain.

Capt Madigan, S/Sgt Loveless and Cpl O'Meara were in the field with the Australian troops until Capt Madigan, who had been slightly wounded, left 11 November for Salamau. Lt Cameron then took over as officer in charge with the same two enlisted men, operating with the 23d Port Headquarters, 41st Infantry Division, at Lae, to cover the Lae -- Finschhafen area. They returned to Headquarters USAFFE 2 December 1943 for duty with one of the other field teams.

The team salvaged all Japanese Ordnance materiel of interest in the area, totaling about 60 tons of weapons (including fifty pieces of artillery) and ninety tons of ammunition. Lae -- Salamaua was the most productive of enemy Ordnance equipment up to the Hollandia operation.

It was reported that there were also large quantities of Chemical Warfare equipment stored in the Salamaua -- Lae area. On 8 September orders were issued attaching Lt Barry and Pfc Going, Chemical Warfare Intelligence Team No. 1, to the 5th Australian Infantry Division, which was operating in the Salamaua area.

It was not thought, however, at this time, that Lae would fall in the near future, and it was anticipated that Team No. 1 would be able to cover the Salamaua area first and then proceed to Lae. In the event that Lae fell prior to the completion of the Salamaua mission, arrangements were made for CWS Intelligence Team No. 2 to proceed to Lae immediately.

During September 1943 operations around Lae were intensified and with the greater part of the available transport planes being used to fly in troops and supplies, transportation for CWS Intelligence Team No. 1 was delayed and they did not arrive in Dobodura until 16 September. Upon arrival, they reported to the United States liaison officer, 1st Australian Corps. It was learned that Lae had fallen that very day and a message was sent to Lt Bond, suggesting that his CWS Team No. 2 proceed there at once. Meanwhile, considerable quantities of enemy Chemical Warfare equipment were found throughout the area by Team No. 1.

HISTORY OF TECHNICAL INTELLIGENCE

After an air raid alarm on the morning of the 20th September, Lt Bond and Pfc Garner, CWS Team No. 2, took off from Ward Drome, Port Moresby, and flew to Nadzab, the closest point to Lae. Upon landing, they reported to the 7th Australian Division which was located a short distance from the field. There, arrangements were made for them to report to 26th Australian Brigade, located in Lae. While they were awaiting transportation to Lae, nine Japanese bombers came over, but mistaking them for friendly planes, no one paid any attention until the anti-aircraft guns opened up over the field. After all this delay transportation was finally secured to Lae.

Capt Forsyth of Advanced Allied Translator and Interpreter section was there with a Japanese interpreter. Lt Brown of Mobile Explosives Investigating Unit (MEIU) United States Navy, was contacted, and also Lt White, who had been transferred with Sgt Bruner from the Ordnance Analysis Section to Ordnance Technical Intelligence, Fifth Air Force.

Shortly after arrival, the team was transferred from the 26th Australian Brigade to Headquarters, 23d Port Detachment, where transportation facilities were more available. After collecting samples of all the Japanese equipment found in the area, Lt Bond and Pfc Garner left Lae on 25th September for Salamaua where they met Lt Barry and Pfc Going of CWS Team No. 1. This team planned to proceed to Lae and from there to Finschhafen as soon as it should fall. All captured equipment collected by CWS Team No. 1 in the Salamaua area was flown by plane from Salamaua back to Dobodura.

On 26 September, transportation by water was obtained to Lae, and Headquarters for CWS Team No. 1 was set up with the 23d Port Headquarters. After a two-day wait for air transportation, Lt Bond and Pfc Garner left for Port Moresby with the equipment collected at Lae and Salamaua.

By this time the cleaning up of Lae had progressed considerably. As at Salamaua, it was again evident that the Japanese had evacuated the area in great haste. Large quantities of documents, ammunition and equipment had been left undestroyed.

Finschhafen: 22 Sep 1943 -- 2 Oct 1943

In a coordinated land, sea and air movement an Australian force moved around the coast from Lae and under cover of heavy air and naval bombardment landed and established beachheads six miles north

of Finschhafen (Map Incl 1) on 22 September 1943. The speed of
the double development of Lae and Finschhafen apparently had
caught the enemy by surprise.

Fierce fighting followed the Allied landing, and in the
latter stages of the operation many hundreds of Japs died of
starvation, wounds and sickness. The capture of Finschhafen
insured Allied control of Huon Gulf, (Map Incl 1) and dislocated
the enemy's grip on British New Guinea.

On 2d October, Lt Barry was notified that Finschhafen had
been occupied and arrangements for transportation to that area
were made immediately. After landing at the wrong beachhead
(which was within five hundred yards of the Japanese position),
Lt Barry and Pfc Going hitch-hiked through the jungle to
Finschhafen, six miles away. Here they attached themselves to
Company A of the 13th Battalion, 20th Australian Brigade, which
was in charge of salvaging enemy equipment in that area.

After recovering all available enemy Chemical Warfare
equipment the team left Finschhafen and returned to Lae and then
back to Nadzab, Dobodura, Port Moresby and finally to Brisbane.

Lt Cameron with S/Sgt Loveless and Cpl O'Meara, who had been
covering the Nassau Bay and Lae areas for captured Ordnance
materiel, operated out of Lae, where they were attached to the
23d Port Headquarters, 41st Division, to cover Finschhafen.

C H A P T E R II

5250th TECHNICAL INTELLIGENCE COMPOSITE COMPANY, SEPARATE PROVISIONAL

January 1944 -- May 1944

On 29 September 1943, all Ordnance personnel were transferred by USAFFE to USASOS, and in late October plans were made by USASOS to provide for a Technical Intelligence Depot consisting of five sections: The original two, Ordnance and Chemical Warfare Service, and in addition, Quartermaster, Medical and Transportation. No detachment was formed, however, for the entire set-up was changed by USAFFE directive, Subject; "Responsibility of Technical Intelligence", dated 22 December 1943, (Incl 6).

By this directive, the responsibility for ground Technical Intelligence within the United States Army Forces in the Far East was delegated to the Commanding General, USASOS. He was directed to appoint qualified officers to serve as United States Army representatives on the Allied Captured Enemy Equipment Board, to provide necessary officer and enlisted personnel to operate the United States Captured Enemy Equipment Depot and to furnish Technical Intelligence personnel both officer and enlisted for inclusion in task force Intelligence teams.

Technical Intelligence operations in SWPA had, in the past, been carried on by detachments of special staff sections operating under varying arrangements in regard to assignment of personnel and supervision of activities. In order to provide an efficient basis for operations of the various Technical Intelligence detachments, USASOS, G-2, Col Sauve', submitted a proposed plan of operation with a recommended T/O and T/E that included, for the first time, the six major services, (all except Transportation Corps) and that was estimated to be adequate for Theater needs, and recommended that a Technical Intelligence Composite Company be activated. This proposal was forwarded to Commanding General USAFFE on 7 December 1943. It was felt that the suggested organization would give more satisfactory Technical Intelligence coverage since it included the six services, that it would make possible the necessary flexibility operation and movement of personnel which was considered essential for the efficient functioning of the sections, and would enable the formation of well trained and balanced Technical Intelligence teams.

Under this arrangement, the several Technical Intelligence sections would be able to facilitate the collection and rapid dissemination of Technical Intelligence information. It would also enable them to control the distribution of captured enemy equipment according to technical and training needs in the Theater and in the United States.

On 3 January 1944, the 5250th Technical Intelligence Composite Company, Separate (Provisional) was organized as a provisional company by General Orders No. 2, Headquarters USASOS (Incl 7), so that assignment of personnel could be made and operations continued. T/O and T/E, previously suggested to USAFFE, were used as guides, with personnel carried on detached service from source units.

The formation of a separate Technical Intelligence Composite Company other than provisional was not favorably considered by USAFFE (10 January 1944).

On 20 January 1944, Chiefs of Services were directed to furnish qualified personnel for assignment on detached service to 5250th Technical Intelligence Composite Company, Separate (Provisional) "to enable the accomplishment of the Technical Intelligence mission" (Incl 8). The transfer of personnel to the 5250th was effected by the six services concerned by February 1944. (A complete roster of all personnel assigned to the 5250th from January 1944, when it was formed, until November 1945, when the 5250th Technical Intelligence Composite Company, Separate (Provisional) had moved forward to Japan, is shown in Incl 9. This inclosure lists the dates each man joined and departed from the Company and the awards that he received).

Evaluation of The Technical Intelligence Setup

The principle of having a coordinating unit for Technical Intelligence proved highly satisfactory in the coming months of the war. Centralized control made it possible for teams from the six services to function as one unit, thus enabling them to aid each other during the first days of an operation when speed was important. Information, documents and equipment could be collected for all branches by all teams, and this equipment assembled in a central spot where it could be sorted and evaluated by the individual service team concerned. Coordination provided flexibility, made for greater ease and efficiency in matter of command, and eliminated the question concerning responsibility and scope of authority.

Most important of all, co-ordination made it possible for the command to have adequately equipped teams formed and trained in time for all operations and assured complete coverage by Technical Intelligence.

There was one very definite drawback, however -- the 5250th Technical Intelligence Company was established only as a provisional organization. This in certain ways, complicated its administration, left its personnel still occupying T/O vacancies in units which they had never worked, made it generally impossible to secure well earned and long deserved promotions, and because the company operated on only a quasi-accepted basis, sometimes ham-strung its efforts when it could have been most effective.

Nevertheless, under the direction of the 5250th Technical Intelligence Composite Company, Separate (Provisional), a comprehensive view of Japanese capabilities was secured and Technical Intelligence entered the period when the work of past years brought in positive results. It was a big step forward.

Organization of the 5250th Tech. Intell. Comp. Co., Sep. (P)

The 5250th was composed of a co-ordination and administration section, and a technical section for each of the six major services. Each Technical section, composed of laboratory and enemy equipment Intelligence teams, operated under the technical supervision of the Chief of Service and under the general supervision of the Assistant Chief of Staff, G-2, USASOS (Organization Chart, Incl 10). Duties, as originally outlined in the recommendation to USAFFE, were followed with only minor modifications. They were as follows:

Company Headquarters

a. Administration of the Company and co-ordination of the activities of the several sections.

b. Company commander on duty in the Office of the AC of S, G-2, USASOS, as Co-ordinator of Technical Intelligence. Major Johnston, Ord, in addition to his other duties, was appointed informally as temporary (without orders) commanding officer of the Company and G-2 Technical Intelligence Co-ordinator.

c. One officer on duty in the Office of the AC of S, G-2, USASOS, to conduct Technical Intelligence liaison with the Allied Translator and Interpreter Section SWPA. This responsibility was first delegated to Lt Col Jones, Chief Engineer Intelligence officer, and was later turned over to his assistant, Lt Girard R. Lowrey.

Service Technical Intelligence Officer

A Technical Intelligence officer in the office of each of the services. His duties were:

a. To advise the Chief of Service on Intelligence matters.

b. To supervise Intelligence activities for the particular service, including training, collection, recording, storage and disposition of captured enemy materiel.

c. To collaborate with the Technical Intelligence sections of other services.

d. To review and issue reports on captured enemy materiel, installations and procedures, and to forward such information to their respective Chiefs of Service in Washington, D. C.

Service Technical Intelligence officers assigned were:

Maj John A. Riddick....... CWS	Maj Alan C. Johnston.... ORD
Lt Col Walter B. Jones.....CE	Maj Murray Herman....... QMC
Maj Steinberg............. MC	No service Intelligence officer
(appointed later, in April)	for Signal Corps.

Administrative and Analysis Unit

Originally, only the Ordnance, Quartermaster and Signal sections operated analysis laboratories under the Chief of the Intelligence Section of the service concerned. Chemical Warfare Service continued to have its analysis work carried on at the 42d Chemical or Victoria Munitions Supply Laboratoies, and Engineer and Medical Corps had no teams in the field until the Hollandia operation in April 1944. Laboratories for all the services were established after that.

HISTORY OF TECHNICAL INTELLIGENCE

All Technical Intelligence sections, however, maintained administrative divisions, which within the scope of their activities:

    a. Advised the Chief of Service on Intelligence matters.

    b. Coordinated and supervised Intelligence activities.

    c. Planned, supervised, and correlated Intelligence training activities.

    d. Established and maintained Intelligence liaison, and collaborated with the Technical Intelligence sections of other arms and services and Allied Forces within the Theater.

    e. Maintained adequate liaison with the Intelligence Division, Office of the Chief of Service.

    f. Interpreted, evaluated and disseminated Intelligence information as prescribed.

    g. Carried on adequate and necessary document research.

    h. Supervised the collection, recording, processing, storage and disposition of captured enemy materiel.

    i. Obtained data on operational performance of captured enemy materiel.

    j. Maintained a file of all reports and data available on Technical Intelligence.

    k. Reviewed and issued reports on captured enemy materiel, installations, procedure, etc.

    l. Arranged for the shipment of selected items of captured enemy materiel to the United States for training and other purposes, as required.

    m. Kept current, and submitted inventories of captured enemy equipment available to the service in the Captured Enemy Equipment Depot or service laboratories, or en route to that depot, or in the advanced areas.

n. Prepared preliminary training manuals on the use of captured enemy equipment, installations, etc., and assisted in planning a training program for United States personnel.

o. Prepared reports of activities of the Section.

Field Teams

Field Teams of each Technical Intelligence Section, within the scope of their activities:

a. Collected and forwarded technical combat information through G-2 of the task force.

b. Arranged for the collection and forwarding of captured enemy equipment to the Service Chief for further analysis or to the Captured Enemy Equipment Depot for shipment to the United States.

c. Assisted and advised G-2 and the appropriate service officer of the task force on all matters of Technical Intelligence.

d. Investigated reports of the use of new methods, weapons, or tactics, and submitted reports thereon through G-2 of the task force.

e. Made preliminary examination of and report on enemy equipment captured by the task force.

f. Cooperated with Technical Intelligence personnel of other services and Allied forces.

g. Assisted in interrogation of prisoners of war when requested to do so.

h. Collected information regarding enemy installations, and prepared reports thereon for forwarding.

i. Arranged for the salvage of bulk supplies and materiel.

j. Submitted reports on captured enemy materiel forwarded to the Captured Enemy Equipment Depot.

k. Maintained current inventories of captured enemy materiel.

HISTORY OF TECHNICAL INTELLIGENCE

Captured Enemy Equipment Depot (QM Intelligence Section)

The Captured Enemy Equipment Depot, which operated directly under the supervision of the Chief Quartermaster Intelligence Section:

a. Received, classified and maintained stock record accounts on all captured enemy equipment forwarded to the Depot.

b. Delivered selected items of captured enemy equipment to the appropriate service or force upon authority received from the Allied Captured Enemy Equipment Board.

c. Packed and shipped to the United States selected items of captured enemy equipment, as directed.

d. Prepared and kept current an inventory of captured enemy equipment and a record of the source and distribution of those items to be forwarded through channels at the proper time.

e. Prepared a monthly report containing a list of captured enemy equipment forwarded to the United States during the month.

f. Returned or forwarded to individuals for souveniring such items as were released on the certificate of the AC of S, G-2, USASOS, or other authorized agencies.

Early Administration by the 5250th Tech. Intell Comp Co. Sep 3 (P).

Lt Orric P. Sell, Jr. was relieved of duty as Commanding Officer of the Depot and as a member of the Allied Enemy Equipment Board when the 5250th was formed and was replaced by Major Murray Herman, QMC.

On 19 February 1944, a directive was received by Headquarters, USASOS, from the Commanding General, USAFFE, to the effect that photographs, prints, rubbings and drawings of all nameplates or nameplate data from all captured enemy equipment would be forwarded to that headquarters. The collection of nameplates and rubbings became one of the main missions of Technical Intelligence personnel. They were to send in literally thousands of those items during the coming months of the war, and from information based on their translation (names, dates, etc.) Japanese manufacturers of war materiel were identified and located -- information that was important in determining air raid targets and in studying the enemy's economic status.

HISTORY OF TECHNICAL INTELLIGENCE

Greater emphasis was also placed on analysis of captured equipment as an additional factor for the determination of the enemy's economic position. Sound deductions as to the state of enemy resources for war could be based on evidence obtained from a laboratory analyses of captured materiel. Technical reports included, when possible, conclusions, positive or negative, as to the enemy's economic status. These conclusions were based on a comparison of material and workmanship of recently and previously captured equipment. When such changes were noted, these items were returned to the United States for further laboratory analysis.

In February 1944 Major Johnston, accompanied by one officer from each of the other six services and 1st Lt James E. Shelby, QMC, proceeded to advanced areas to inform base sections and army troops that as each of the six services were interested in materiel, all captured Japanese equipment was desired and should be forwarded. At the same time he informed personnel of the modification of the regulation that facilitated legitimate souveniring. (It was hoped that this would encourage troops to turn in captured equipment, though it turned out that it had little effect on the willful looting and destruction of enemy dumps.) Major Johnston also informed forward echelons of the proceedure necessary for shipment of captured materiel.

Captain Madigan, having returned from field detail in the Nassau Bay, Lae and Finschhafen areas, had departed on 17 November 1943 for temporary duty to the Office of the Chief of Ordnance, Washington, D. C. This was in conformity with War Department policy of having personnel of Technical Intelligence teams on temporary duty from the War Department return periodically for consultation. He was gone until 30 March 1944 when he returned to report that great interest had been aroused in the Army Service Forces, Washington, D. C., in Technical Intelligence and that numerous conferences concerning the enemy materiel situation were held.

At the same time Captain Madigan left for Washington, permission was requested from the Chief of Ordnance to have Captain Edward I. Creed, who was assigned to Ordnance Intelligence activities in the Alaskan area, sent to the Southwest Pacific for duty with Ordnance Intelligence. On 15 December 1943 Headquarters Ordnance Intelligence Section was notified that Captain Creed would proceed to Washington for six weeks temporary duty and then would be sent to this Theater.

19

HISTORY OF TECHNICAL INTELLIGENCE

Saidor: 2 Jan 1944 -- 10 Feb 1944

In December 1943 a request had been sent to G-2, USAFFE, to arrange with Sixth Army to have a combined Technical Intelligence Field Unit participate in the Cape Gloucester operation. However, after receiving permission from Sixth Army, the unit upon arrival at Finschhafen was not allowed to go forward. An officer and two enlisted men, however, did secure permission to go on the Saidor (Map Incl 1) operation 2 January 1944, though the combined unit was not used. Lt Bishop, T/4 Winn and Cpl Beveridge, who had operated as an Ordnance Intelligence Team with the 32d Division since 20 October 1943, participated on this and minor operations up the New Guinea coast (Map Incl 1). From information secured, the team prepared a small booklet as an amplification of the Allied Land Force Headquarters pamphlet on Japanese equipment.

They also assisted in the staging program of the 32d Division on Goodenough Island, instructing the troops on booby traps and enemy Ordnance materiel. It was found more and more that such training of combat troops in use of Japanese weapons, especially small arms and machine guns, was of considerable value to the task force.

The team remained at Saidor until March 1944, when they were relieved. Lt Bishop and T/4 Winn were then attached to the 41st Infantry Division for the Hollandia operation.

Admiralty Islands: 29 Feb 1944 -- 18 May 1944

The invasion of the Admiralty Islands (Maps Incls 1 and 11) specifically Momote Airstrip on Los Negros, was begun 29 February 1944, when the enemy was caught completely off guard in a surprise landing.

The campaign marked the final stage in the great swinging movement, pivoting on New Guinea, which had been the basic plan of operations in the Southwest Pacific.

Men of the First Cavalry Division landed on Manus Island about one and a half miles northwest of Lorengau, (Map Incl 11) on 15 March. They were covered by artillery fire from small neighboring islands seized the day before, and were supported by destroyers, P. T. boats and air bombardment. Brushing aside the initial light opposition, the force divided, one group heading toward the airstrip, the other branching off to the south.

HISTORY OF TECHNICAL INTELLIGENCE

Within three days after their landing on Manus Island United States Cavalrymen captured Lorengau airstrip, and on 18 March they stormed their way into Lorengau town. They then had occupied all vital areas in the Admiralty Islands.

The chief prize of the Admiralty victory was Sea Eagle Harbor, (Map Incl 11) which had 55 miles of protected waterway formed by a lagoon of several islands and reefs. It and the two strategic airstrips at Lorengau on Manus Island and Momote on Los Negros, formed a potential base for intensive operations against the remaining enemy strongholds in New Britain and New Ireland (Map Incl 1).

As originally planned in November 1943, and attempted for Cape Gloucester, Technical Intelligence field operations were to be based on the principle of assigning a field unit composed of one officer and two enlisted men each to a Counter Intelligence team for each task force. This provided for collection and investigation of enemy materiel at the earliest possible moment after combat operations.

In accordance with this plan it was decided that a combined Ordnance and Chemical Warfare Service unit should accompany the 1st Cavalry Division in the Admiralties campaign. (The other four services did not have trained personnel available for field operations until the Hollandia operation in April 1944). A Counter Intelligence Corps (CIC) officer was to be in charge of the unit and consolidated reports were to be forwarded covering Counter Intelligence, Ordnance, Chemical Warfare Service, and Naval Mobile Explosive Investigation Unit (MEIU) No. 1 activities. Captured documents were to be forwarded to Allied Translator and Interpreter Section. The CIC team consisted of one officer, 1st Lt Harold F. Frederick, and eight enlisted men. Technical Intelligence personnel consisted of one officer, Lt Cameron, and two enlisted men, S/Sgt Loveless and Sgt Lischalk, of the Ordnance Section; one officer, Lt Henry, and two enlisted men, Pfc Gaddo and Pvt Street, of the Chemical Warfare Intelligence Section. Also as part of the unit were one Naval officer, Lt Bushnell, and one enlisted man from MEIU No. 1. The group was organized and fully equipped by G-2, USAFFE, before being sent to join the 1st Cavalry Division. Lt Frederick was placed in command of all personnel, including Technical Intelligence. They functioned as a unit with success during the entire Admiralty Islands campaign.

HISTORY OF TECHNICAL INTELLIGENCE

Lt Frederick and Sgt Anderson (CIC), Lt Bushnell, MEIU (Navy), and Lt Henry (CWS) and Sgt Lischalk (Ord) composed the first section of the unit to leave for the Admiralties. They were attached to the S-2 of the 12th Cavalry Regiment to accompany them to Los Negros where they were to reinforce the 5th Cavalry Regiment, then in combat. The departure was delayed for two days and during this time Lt Henry assisted in preparing a geographic survey of Los Negros to be used by the regiment. The information thus obtained proved invaluable on later patrols.

The group departed from Cape Sudest, New Guinea, (Map Incl 1) so as to arrive at Hyane Harbor, Los Negros, (Map Incl 11) on the 6th of March, (D plus 6). Although the crisis of the operation had passed, the area cleared by the troops was yet very small. This enabled the team to arrive at captured equipment and materiel dumps before they had been pillaged and souvenired. Lt Henry and Sgt Lischalk joined the 1st Cavalry Division Headquarters at Sea Eagle Harbor. The top ranking officers of the Division were interested in Technical Intelligence, were anxious that the team should start immediately, and saw to it that it was provided with necessary equipment.

During subsequent action, materiel and documents were received in great quantities, and cooperation from the line units and individual soldiers was splendid. They gave information as to the location of dumps and brought in quantities of materiel. The lectures and demonstrations to the troops on the value of enemy equipment for Intelligence purposes paid high dividends.

On 9 March, Lt Cameron and Sgt Loveless arrived. A collection dump was organized and the first bulk shipment of captured materiel was shipped from Hyane Harbor.

The remainder of the detachment arrived 16 March. Pfc Gaddo was immediately utilized in following the assault back of Papitalai Mission (Map Incl 11) where a Chemical dump had been reported. Pvt Street was kept busy with photographic work for the detachment and the Division G-2. Both men were subsequently used on patrols, and continued with this until the end of the campaign.

The dumps located consisted of weapons, ammunition, quartermaster items, and medical supplies of all kinds. Many small dumps were located a few yards off the trail, protected and camouflaged by canvas, grass, or metal roofing. Each dump was usually of one class of supplies such as clothing, medical supplies or one type of ammunition. Chemical Warfare protection equipment and munitions were found in this sector.

HISTORY OF TECHNICAL INTELLIGENCE

All the documents and equipment were assembled but no attempt was made to sort the materiel in respect to services until it had reached the collecting area. In this connection, transportation was the critical factor. Not only was land transportation needed, but due to the insular nature of the campaign, water transportation also had to be available.

The problem was met by utilizing the trucks hauling supplies. When empty and ready to go back to the beachhead, captured equipment was loaded aboard and was taken as far as the beach. By the same procedure with the landing craft, the materiel was eventually returned to headquarters. This method of back loading for bulk shipments, though effective, was slow, and caused considerable loss of time. Shipping back to the Depot at Brisbane offered little trouble, since, with the exception of the first difficulty, rush shipments were made by back-loading aircraft.

Photographs were taken, developed and printed of all new types of equipment, fortifications, and operations in so far as possible. It was found that due to the heat and lack of proper washing facilities for the negatives and prints, photographic work was difficult under field conditions. Later it was found advantageous to wait and send exposed film to photographic laboratories for developing and printing.

This was the first campaign in which the various services were coordinated, and it confirmed the fact that by combining their efforts they could cover more territory in less time. Only Chemical Warfare Service and Ordnance pooled their work for this operation but their success substantiated the decision to combine all six services for the Hollandia operation.

By May 1944 all important areas in the Admiralty Islands had been searched and all materiel of value had been collected and shipped. The Unit had completed its mission and the personnel returned to their various organizations.

C H A P T E R   III

HOLLANDIA

April 1944 -- July 1944

To trap the 18th Japanese Army dispersed along the coast of New Guinea and to capture suitable air bases for the future offensive against the Philippines, the Allies hurdled the stretch of northern New Guinea coast from Saidor to Hollandia. The map of New Guinea had suggested the five hundred mile hop. The Japanese response to our feints at Wewak and Madang, (Map Incl 1) 205 and 385 miles below Hollandia, had invited it.

It was a big step, and plans were laid to use the greatest force yet assembled in the Southwest Pacific -- two United States Army divisions -- to be involved in a single operation. It was furthermore, the first all-American show in the Pacific.

Staging for the Hollandia Operation

Technical Intelligence was to give complete coverage of this operation, for it was known that Hollandia (Map Incl 12) was one of the important Japanese supply installations for Southeastern New Guinea and New Britain defensive areas. Indicative of the fact that Technical Intelligence was still in a formative stage, organizationally speaking, were the various modes of operation used. Three teams and one composite unit were to go in during the initial stages of the battle -- one team operating free lance, one team in a combined detachment patterned after that used for the Admiralties campaign, and one composite unit representing all six services. This last, the Composite Technical Intelligence Unit, was an innovation, that laid the basis for organization of Technical Intelligence teams for the balance of the Japanese war.

CWS Team No. 2 (Lt Bond and T/5 Going) and the Ordnance Technical Intelligence Team composed of Lt Bishop and Cpl Winn were both attached to the 41st Division, but were in no combined team during this operation. The CWS Team had not been in an operation since Salamaua, but the Ordnance team had been replaced from duty with the 32d Division after the close of the Saidor operation, just in time to join the 41st Division at Finschhafen in March to stage for Hollandia.

Chemical Warfare Service Team No. 6 and a Mobile Explosives Investigation Unit, were attached to Combat Team B of the Counter Intelligence Corps in a combined detachment similar to that used in the Admiralties. The group was attached to the Office of the AC of S, G-2, 24th Infantry Division.

CWS Team No. 6 composed of 2d Lt Allen W. Phillips, and Pvt John Kruger, who had been added to the original CWS Technical Intelligence personnel, went into staging early in January for this operation. The staging area, on Goodenough Island, forward echelon of the 24th Infantry Division was New Guinea. Here, the team assisted in the training program, presenting lectures on Technical Intelligence to all units in the Division that missed it on the mainland. This lecture series was coordinated with the CIC training program.

While in the staging area, a plan for establishment of a divisional captured enemy equipment depot was submitted to the G-2 of the Division. This was accepted and a memo was sent to all units, outlining channels for forwarding captured enemy equipment to this central collection point.

First Composite Unit is Formed for Hollandia Operation

Major Riddick, CWS, Major Talcott Wainwright, MC, (now with 5250th), Major Madigan, Ord (who had been recently promoted), and Lt. Rowe, Signal, arrived at Finschhafen from Brisbane 13 April to start things rolling for staging Technical Intelligence Unit No. 1 for Hollandia.

During that week the following personnel arrived at Finschhafen to join the unit: 1st Lt Bob C. Woodson, Transportation Corps; Capt William H. Lambert and fourteen enlisted men · from the 234th Quartermaster Salvage Collecting Company — these men were not Technical Intelligence personnel but were to accompany the Unit on the operation; and Lt Barry from CWS Team No. 1, who was hospitalized as soon as he arrived — he recovered just in time to accompany the Unit on the operation.

HISTORY OF TECHNICAL INTELLIGENCE

On 22 April 1944, four officers recently attached to the
Pacific theater from the Military Intelligence Training Center
at Camp Ritchie, Maryland, arrived: Captain Eugene H. Manley,
CE, and 2d Lt Philip N. Van Slyck, Ord, who were trained for
Combat Intelligence; 1st Lt Guy N. Birleffi, Ord, and 2d Lt
Jerry A. Ricci, QC, who were trained in interrogation of
prisoners of war. The last one to join the Unit was 1st Lt
Edward S. Peck, CE, who arrived 23 April.

During the staging period, the following supplies typical
of those taken into the field by Technical Intelligence teams
were drawn: Jungle clothing, field equipment, office supplies,
Ordnance, ammunition, wrapping materials. Training was given
to unit members on identification of Japanese materiel, especially Ordnance and Chemical Warfare Service, with Major
Riddick initiating the instruction and Major Madigan reviewing
and amplifying the information on Ordnance. Major Wainwright
discussed tropical diseases, health and sanitation in the
jungle, with emphasis on prevention of malaria and typhus.

The day that Capt Manley and his group arrived, personnel
were informed of the task force objective and were shown landing
points and probable locations of enemy troops and dumps. The
following day Col Sauve' arrived from Brisbane to discuss pre-
movement plans.

The unit was not to go in on the operation until D plus
8. (30 April). On 25 April at 2000 they were alerted. After
a 2½ ton truck, two jeeps and two ¼ ton trailers in a pouring
rain, the unit had to scour the base for a dispersing gas dump,
and reached embarkation beach at 0200. Unable to secure permission to board, they slept in their vehicles the rest of the
night. The following day, loading was again held up and the
group returned to their own area to await development.

Finally, at about 1700 hours on 27 April, everyone except
Lt Ricci, who was to take over administration of the United
States Army Technical Intelligence Depot that was to be set up
at Finschhafen, Pvts Abraham and Ogle, who were assigned as
Depot personnel, and Lt Birleffi, who was left as the rear
echelon for the Unit to bring up vehicles and personal baggage
later, boarded an LST and proceded in convoy toward Hollandia,
arriving on D plus 8.

Operations at Hollandia

Covering a front of about 120 miles, ground troops hit the beaches at Aitape, Hollandia and Tanahmerah Bay, (Map Incl 12) on 22 April. 1 Corps directed operations with a combined Task Force consisting of the 41st Infantry Division, landing at Humboldt Bay, (Map Incl 12) and the 24th Infantry Division, landing at Tanahmerah Bay. Simultaneously, 120 miles southeast, a separate Task Force, the 163d Regimental Combat Team (part of the 41st Infantry Division), landed at Aitape.

The Hollandia, Humboldt Bay and Tanahmerah Bay areas were primarily supply installations and were lacking in anti-invasion and coastal defense positions. The areas did have, however, anti-aircraft gun batteries and elaborate air raid shelters typical of Japanese forward area bases.

H hour was scheduled for 0700. The naval bombardment began at 0600 hours and was lifted shortly before the first wave hit the beaches. No opposition was met in any sector and the only fire received came from small caliber weapons which were quickly silenced by destroyers standing off shore.

It was a quick and decisive Allied victory. The primary objective had been the seizure of the Cyclops, Sentani and Hollandia airdromes, (Map Incl 13) and by the 24th April, little more than two days after the initial landings, infantrymen had captured all three airdromes and were scouring the hills north of Lake Sentani (Map Incl 13) for signs of the retreating enemy.

Lt Bishop and Cpl Winn landed on D Day at Humboldt Bay, White Beach 1, with the assault troops of the 41st Division. There were many large dump areas along the shore and a temporary captured equipment dump was set up on the beach. The team bivouaced with the 741st Ordnance Company that first night just off White Beach 1. The second day was spent in reconnaisance of the area toward the town of Hollandia. Considerable materiel was recovered both in the open and also stored in caves along the sides of the hills. However, the distance was too great and no materiel was evacuated to the dump on this day.

The team returned to the original bivouac area that night, and on that night -- D plus one -- a single Jap bomber dropped three bombs into the area. Two of the bombs landed in the middle of the ammunition and gasoline that had been unloaded on the beach. Approximately $5,000,000 worth of supplies were blown up that night. One-tenth of a second later they would have missed the supply dump, for the third bomb landed on top of the cliff beyond the beach and did little damage. Down the beach everyone dove for caves. Burning gasoline and oil spread to the ammunition, fires burned furiously, and ammunition was detonating all through the night. The explosions were terrific. Not many slept that night.

Following the destruction of the food supply, rations were cut one-third, later to one meal a day. The Task Force at Hollandia was 500 miles deep into enemy country, the Japanese held the coast and supplies were going fast.

On D plus three Lt Bishop and Cpl Winn moved to Pim Jetty where the 186th Infantry was proceeding toward the three airdromes. This area was selected because the road was open through to the dromes and the danger of troops moving in and souveniring before Technical Intelligence could recover the materiel was great, whereas the Hollandia area itself could only be reached by barge. It was felt that the materiel in Hollandia would be safe from souveniring till the team could get at it in the future. As it worked out, they were even then late in getting along the Pim Jetty motor track as all the dumps had been tampered with and nearly all the boxes opened and the contents scattered.

Due to road conditions, only an inspection trip was made by the teams into the airdrome area. Outside of the anti-aircraft guns at the strips, most of the materiel was of Air Corps origin. There were a great many wrecked airplanes on the strips indicating the thoroughness of the pre-invasion bombing. Along the road the fuel dumps had been set on fire by strafing attacks as shown by spent United States 50 caliber machine gun bullets. After this area was covered the team moved to the town of Hollandia where the 162d Infantry was located.

On D plus 8, Major Madigan arrived with the Technical Intelligence Composite Unit No. 1 and all Ordnance activities were placed under his supervision.

By the time CWS Team No. 6 together with the MEIU and the CIC Team, arrived on Red Beach 2, of Tanahmerah Bay with elements of the 24th Infantry Division several enemy outposts had been discovered in the beach area which gave evidence of hasty evacuation. Terrain difficulties between Red Beach 2 and the advancing infantry prevented adequate supplies reaching them and necessitated moving the Division Command Post to Red Beach 1. This was accomplished on D plus 1. On arriving at Red Beach 1, CWS Team No. 6 (Lt Phillips and Pvt Kruger) found it impractical to continue toward the air drome -- a landslide had considerably increased the supply problem and the rains of the previous nights had made movement by truck impossible. In the vicinity of Red Beach 1, several more outposts were located and searched, resulting in the discovery of more equipment.

Shortly after the Hollandia drome had been taken, the first enemy supply dumps were located approximately three miles northwest of the dromes. This was co-incident with the appearance of the first semblance of a road seen so far.

The morning of D plus 5, Lt Phillips and Pvt Kruger accompanied a patrol which contacted a patrol from the 41st Infantry Division between Sentani and Hollandia air dromes. Around midday CWS Team No. 6 met CWS Team No. 2 (Lt Pond and T/5 Going) attached to the 41st Infantry Division and learned that large quantities of enemy equipment had been captured in the area.

The fact that there was no transportation available from the 24th Division and the apparent absence of Chemical equipment in the Division's area, prompted CWS Team No. 6 to join CWS Team No. 2 in order to expedite coverage of the large storage areas captured in the 41st Division sector.

During the period 28 April to 7 May, CWS Team No. 6 worked continually with CWS Team No. 2 in the 41st Division Sector. Contact was maintained with the G-2, 24th Infantry Division, but finally on 8 May CWS Team No. 6 reported back to the Command Post. By this time, Technical Intelligence Composite Unit No. 1 had arrived in the operations area to take over the enemy equipment thus far collected. It was planned for this Composite Unit to handle any Technical Intelligence functions that might arise in the future and for CWS Team No. 6 to be made available for a future operation. On 9 May CWS Team No. 6 left Hollandia and reported back to Headquarters USASOS.

Technical Intelligence Composite Unit No. 1 came in on an LST on White Beach 1, Humboldt Bay, Hollandia section, on D plus 8, the 30th of April. The personnel assisted the troops in discharging cargo, pending the arrival of labor troops. All stores were stacked on the beach twenty-five yards off shore, for want of transportation to a safer disposal area.

HISTORY OF TECHNICAL INTELLIGENCE

The day they landed Major Riddick became ill and was returned to Finchhafen Major Wainwright assumed command of the Unit.

Without proper orders and adequate authorization, the Unit ran into the old problem of determining their status and formulating plans for action. Considerable time was lost by Major Wainwright's having to go into conference with 2d Port Headquarters advance echelon and representatives of Reckless Task Force so that the status of the Unit could be established.

A temporary camp site for the Unit was located on the beach under a bluff occupied by a battery of 40 mm AA. A storage tent and jungle hammocks were erected, but no attempt was made to set up a permanent camp site.

The first two days, personnel reconnoitered for Japanese dumps on the trail to Hollandia town, at White Beach 3 and on Jautefa Bay. Lt Van Slyck and Cpl Turves received permission to go to Sawmill Jetty with a light machine gun squad from the 532d Boat and Shore Regiment reinforcing a rifle squad from the 24th Infantry holding the jetty and the beach. On the excursion that took them into Waak Village, several hundred enemy dumps of clothing, food and medical supplies were located.

The second night, around 2000 hours, two Japanese single engine planes came directly over the beach supply and camp site area at about 700 feet and dropped high explosives and anti-personnel bombs, two of which straddled the camp area, the rest landing on top of the bluff, wiping out the AA battery. The number of killed and wounded from this bombing attack exceeded that from the previous one on D plus 1 when so much destruction was caused to the supplies. However, no one in the Unit suffered injuries.

Much of the Unit's clothing and equipment was blown up. For days after that they had nothing to wear except what they had on their backs or could salvage from Jap dumps. Meantime, the food shortage caused by the original destruction of the supply dump on D plus one continued.

As arrangements by Major Wainwright with G-4 of the Task Force the day before the bombing the camp was moved to Brinkman's Plantation, southwest of Pim Jetty on Jautefa Bay. Lt Peck moved equipment by LCV to the new camp site which was in the vicinity of I Corps Signal dump and Major Madigan supervised setting up the camp -- two tents for quarters and a native building for storage located in a grassy area in a kapok grove.

That night there was another air raid alert. Planes were sighted, but no bombs were dropped.

The next day things got under way: Major Wainwright procured authorization from Task Force G-2 for members of the Technical Intelligence Composite Unit to enter Japanese dumps and remove equipment of Intelligence value; Major Madigan established liaison with I Corps Ordnance for assistance in recovering equipment and he also procured additional space near the camp site as an Ordnance storage area; Lt Rowe established liaison with I Corps Signal Office for assistance in collecting Signal equipment.

In the following days Major Wainwright located large Medical dumps; Major Madigan took over large quantities of captured Ordnance which had been collected by combat troops and together with Lt Van Slyck and Cpl Tarves evacuated additional Japanese equipment. Lt Rowe located items of Signal Intelligence value; Capt Lambert brought in supplies of Japanese clothing and food. Lt Van Slyck, Lt Woodson, and Lt Birleffi collected CWS materiel.

Nearly all the items recovered in the Hollandia areas were in the original packing and in fine shape, as left by the Japanese. However, quantities of materiel were destroyed by United States Army souvenir hunters. Dumps were ransacked, cases opened and many complete machine shops were ruined by souvenir hunters picking them apart. Nevertheless, tons of enemy equipment of all kinds were recovered by the teams -- more than on any previous operation -- and much of this equipment was of high Intelligence value.

Among the other captured documents, a rather interesting Japanese propaganda magazine printed in English, Malay and Japanese, reporting on the success of "Greater East Asia Co-prosperity Sphere", was turned over by the Unit to the CIC for translation and disposition by ATIS.

From time to time several changes in assignment of personnel were made: Lt Van Slyck was appointed temporary troop commander; Lt Peck was returned to Finschhafen and en route assisted in procuring water transportation for the Unit; Major Riddick who had recovered from his illness, Lt Birelffi and Pvt Ogle rejoined the Unit, having come up from Finschhafen on the Dutch ship, Janssens with two weapons carriers and a one-ton trailer; Major Riddick took over command from Major Wainwright, who, having

secured five cases of Japanese Medical equipment with three
samples of each item, terminated his detached service and flew
to Brisbane, Australia, with the equipment to have it translated
and analyzed and to report results of Medical Technical Intelligence to Col Sauve'; Pvt John Kruger, newly assigned to 5250th
from C/S section 41st Division, joined the Unit; T/5 Paul R.
Going was released from the Unit to accompany Lt Bond, C/S Team
No. 2, serving with the 41st Division. Lt Rowe left on temporary
duty with United States Forces at Biak, (Map Incl 12) to pro-
cure Signal Intelligence materiel in that area, his mission at
Hollandia completed, he procured orders for himself from Sixth
Army, saw to it that all his equipment collected in the Hollandia
area was packed, crated and labelled, ready for shipment, and
made arrangements with I Corps transportation for shipment.

On 20 May, G-2 USASOS directed the following appointments:

Major Madigan.......................Executive
Capt Manley........................Adjutant
Capt Lambert......................Troop Commander
Lt Van Slyck......................Area Commandant
Lt Birleffi......................Transportation Officer
Lt Woodson......................Mess Officer
Lt Van Slyck......................Supply Officer
Capt Lambert......................Depot Officer
Lt Van Slyck......................Assistant Depot Officer

The Unit had the usual trouble with the misappropriation of
property; the two weapons carriers and the one-ton trailer,
brought up from Finschhafen by Major Riddick and Lt Birleffi was
discharged by mistake at White Beach 1. When finally located
by Lt Birleffi, one weapons carrier had been taken over by a
Signal unit and both truck and trailer had been looted. Report
was made first to Inspecting General, I Corps, then to Commanding General, Base G.

A captured Ordnance equipment dump set up by Major Madigan
at Brinkman's Plantation with materiel crated and stenciled for
shipment to the United States, was removed without authority by
194th Ordnance Battalion. Letter reporting the incident was
sent to I Corps and later to the Commanding General, Base G.

Before much improvement was made in the area to better the
health and sanitation conditions, Hollandia was infested with the
usual jungle diseases. In the course of three weeks, nine enlisted men and an officer from the 234th Quartermaster Salvage

There were, in addition, two other casualties sustained by Unit members: 1st Sgt Chichester was burned with carbolic acid while unloading a truck and was hospitalized; and Capt Lambert was hospitalized for bone fractures and returned to Finschhafen as the result of a collision with a 2½ ton amphibious truck.

Toward the end of May the Unit moved to Kajoabi Delta, just evacuated by C Company of the 842d Aviation Engineer Battalion that was to be the site of the future Technical Intelligence Depot at Hollandia. The area was high, gravelly, shaded, had no undergrowth, had good drainage, and was ample for the Units requirements.

Here a display of captured enemy equipment was set up for visiting officers in a white Japanese tent and two pyramidals.

Shortly after the Unit had settled in their new area, a cloud burst filled and partially dammed the arm of Kojeobi Delta and nearly flooded the Unit out. All hands worked at clearing obstructions in the river bed and in damming the river banks. They saved the area before any damage was done.

Engineer Team No. 3, commanded by Capt Donald D. Connors, was the first Technical Intelligence Engineering team in the field. It was composed of S/Sgt Richard T. Smith and T/4 Roger Sherwood who were relieved from Distribution Division at Intermediate Section, USASOS and were sent to meet Captain Connors, requisitioned from USASOS Engineer at Hollandia on 5 June 1944.

The team inspected the dump areas in Hollandia but found little enemy equipment. Hearing that quantities of enemy Engineering equipment especially certain mobile water purifying units were being recovered at Biak, the team departed a week later for that area.

On 19 June Lt Birleffi went on temporary duty to Finschhafen to inspect and inventory equipment in the Technical Intelligence Depot. On the same day, Lt Stanger, Depot Officer at Finschhafen, arrived at Hollandia to clarify the status of equipment in the field depots there and to reach an understanding on its disposition. He took back with him several items of Japanese equipment and uniforms for a display purpose at the Finschhafen Depot.

The following day Capt Manley, who had been appointed Assistant Coordinator of Technical Intelligence in the Office of the AC of S, G-2, USASOS, left by air for Brisbane, Australia, Lt Van Slyck was appointed Adjutant in his place and Lt Trier was appointed Area Commander vice Lt Van Slyck.

HISTORY OF TECHNICAL INTELLIGENCE

The following personnel, who had previously been requisition-ed from the Chief Chemical Officer, USASOS, joined the Unit 22 June:

1st Lt Otis M. Trier, CWS	T/5 Gasparo Mangiarcina
2d Lt Victor Del Guercio, CWS	Pfc Edgar G. Mulligan
Cpl Nathan H. Anderson	Pvt Edward T. McVerry
T/4 Robert J. Showman (appointed Unit Clerk)	

Toward the end of June there was increased enemy activity in the vicinity, and though no one in the Composite Unit was in-jured, all personnel were directed to be armed when leaving the area.

Because the unit was operating informally, there was some question pertaining to the efficiency of the unit in performing its mission.

On 7 July Lt Pierce Butler III, CE arrived and was appointed the Depot Commander vice Capt Lambert relieved, on 10 July and 11 July the following personnel arrived and were attached to the Depot:

CWS

1st Lt Louis Mecny	T/5 John W. Wargo
2d Lt Lawrence R. Smith	T/5 Thomas J. Irony
M/Sgt Benjamin Booker	T/5 George Griggs
T/Sgt Robert L. Jackson	T/5 Glen A. Glosnoe
T/3 Harold J. Arro	T/5 Carl H. Johnson
T/3 Archie M. Daniel	Pfc George R. Hammerling
T/3 John E. Millard	Pfc Ralph F. Rolott
T/4 Thomas E. Green	Pfc Louis C. Gorzesak
T/4 Howard H. Halbeck	Pfc Theophilis G. Haggis
T/4 James J. McEvoy	Pvt Nathaniel C. Buckley
T/5 Charles T. Test	

ORD

Pfc Albert L. Morath	Pvt Nick P. Vannucci
Pfc Robert M. De Frietas	Pvt Richard E. Reynolds

About the same time Major Riddick was relieved for another assignment and Major Madigan assumed command of the Unit and general supervision of the Depot.

The following day Major Johnston, Coordinator of Technical Intelligence USASOS, arrived to survey the work that had been accomplished by the Unit and to advise the personnel that captured materiel would largely be shipped from Base F, and Base G would be principally a transshipment depot. That day, Major Madigan, Major Shull, Major Johnston, Lt Murphy and Lt Butler conferred with General Yeager on the disposition of the Unit, now that most of the enemy equipment in the area had been recovered.

Major Madigan having completed his mission, returned to Brisbane for conference with the Chief Ordnance Officer, USASOS. On 9 October he reported to Base F to assume charge of the Ordnance Analysis Section of the Technical Intelligence Depot.

CHAPTER IV

BIAK TO MOROTAI

April 1944 -- October 1944

As the war moved forward it gained momentum and scope.
The opening of the Admiralty Islands campaign in February 1944
stretched the lines of communication with headquarters at
Brisbane to 2,000 miles -- a long ways by convoy. For Technical Intelligence, the rapidity of collection and processing
of captured enemy materiel and dissemination of information
is one of the prime missions. The United States Captured
Enemy Equipment Depot at Brisbane was dropping too far behind
the front lines.

The Technical Intelligence Depot Is Moved to Finschhafen

In accordance with letter GSB 323.3 Headquarters USASOS,
25 March 1944 and letter FEGB 386.3 Headquarters USAFFE, 28
March 1944, authority was granted to establish the United
States Army Technical Intelligence Depot at Finschhafen,
effective 20 April 1944.

A warehouse turned over by the base Chemical Warfare Service was converted for use as the Depot building. Walls for
the building were constructed and it was made rain and burglar-
proof.

Lt Ricci, who had been left in charge of the Depot when
the Composite Unit staged for Hollandia in April was relieved of
duty with the 5250th Technical Intelligence Company shortly
afterwards and 1st Lt Edward R. Stangler, AGD, was appointed
Depot Officer.

During July and August the analysis laboratories of the
Technical Intelligence sections were moved from Brisbane to
Finschhafen. At first, the sections utilized the facilities
of the base for their analysis laboratories, and for quarters
for their personnel. This combining of the analysis sections

with the receiving and shipping Depot -- both at the main Depot
at Finschhafen and the temporary field depot at Hollandia -- was
a new and more efficient set-up. It centralized control eliminated certain phases of duplicate administration and handling of
equipment and personnel and was conducive to greater collaboration
among the services.

Lt Alcide Santilli, SC, operated the Signal analysis laboratory at Brisbane until the end of May, when he departed for
Finschhafen to make arrangements for the change in location of
the analysis laboratory and to dispose of captured equipment
that had accumulated there. T/5 Blackledge and T/5 Traub, who
had packed some 2,000 pounds of organization impedimenta for
the move from Brisbane to Finschhafen, worked overtime with
other depot personnel at Finschhafen to expedite the shipment of
captured enemy equipment that had stocked up there from the
Hollandia, Biak, Arara, Wakde, and Sarmi operations.

It was planned that the United States Army Technical Intelligence Depot would not only be a center for the analysis and shipment of captured materiel but also the location for a training
school for orientation of new personnel assigned to Technical
Intelligence duties. Among the first to receive this instruction were 1st Lt Jack M. Daniels and 2d Lt Jacob Overholt, assigned to the 5250th in June and sent forward to the Depot at Base
F shortly afterwards to be briefed by Lt Santilli in methods
of collecting and evaluating enemy Signal materiel on operations with field teams. Briefing included study of technical
data and identification photographs, with emphasis laid on
correct method of reporting, particularly in the matter of
supplying complete information on the place and circumstance of
recovering equipment.

Lt Col William A. Bergin, Signal Corps, made a special trip
to Melbourne to contact the Master General of Ordnance, Australian
Army, in regard to securing samples of captured Japanese Signal
Corps equipment which had been reported in the Australian depot
there.

General Brehon Somervell, Commanding General Army Service
Forces, had offered the services of Army Service Forces enemy
equipment specialists to the Pacific Theater earlier in the year,
and had received immediate concurrence that they were desired.
In March, General Somervell wrote a letter (Incl 14) that clearly established the status of Technical Intelligence specialists
on temporary duty to the theater, and re-emphasized the importance
of Technical Intelligence in the war effort. This personnel was
delayed in arriving until the summer of 1944.

During that summer of 1944, considerable emphasis was
placed on the dissemination of information pertaining to captured enemy equipment. Major Wainwright, returned from the
Hollandia operation, prepared a written report on the analysis
of some hundreds of Japanese Medical items, and edited the
report as Medical Intelligence Booklet No. 1. The booklet was
preliminary and incomplete, but it was thought desirable to pub-
lish it immediately in order to disseminate the information to
the personnel concerned with the least possible delay. Twelve
thousand copies were printed and distributed to Medical field
personnel for use in identifying Japanese drugs and medicines.
The booklet was later made more complete as a result of a trip
by Captain Ulmen O. Clements, to Hollandia in July to bring
back a considerable quantity of Medical material captured on
that operation for analysis in the laboratories in Brisbane.

Publications were also issued by the other services;
Lt Bond made arrangements for printing a Chemical Warfare Technical Intelligence manual; Capt Wilkes assembled data on Japanese weapons; Lt Col Jones prepared and issued three Technical
Intelligence reports for Engineers before he returned to the
United States in September and Capt Connors took over his position in the Office of the Chief Engineer.

Liaison was also maintained with Washington -- Lt Bishop
proceeded to Aberdeen Proving Grounds, Maryland, to submit a
verbal report on Ordnance Technical Intelligence just as Major
Madigan had done half a year before.

A ten-man labor detail was loaned daily to the Depot from
the Base, for with the great increase of captured equipment to
be handled, with increased shipping, tagging, crating, administrative details and many other functions, the need for additional help became urgent. Both officer and enlisted men were added
for duty at Headquarters, at the Depot and with the field teams.
The nucleus of original personnel assigned to the 5250th Technical Intelligence Company expanded.

Arara, Wakde, Sarmi: 17 May -- 2 Sep 1944

Back in the ambitious days of Japanese conquest, the enemy
had developed the Sarmi coastline (Map Incl 12 and 13) as a staging zone for aircraft and supplies directed to the more easterly
bases in New Guinea.

When Hollandia was captured by the Allies in April, there were signs that the two airdromes, one at Maffin Bay and the other at Sawar whose construction had never been fully completed, might be built up for general operations and the whole area converted into a defense sector.

This threat was nipped with the surprise landing at Arara by the 163d Regimental Combat Team (RCT) of the 41st Infantry Division on 17 May 1944. Two days later the Japs lost the Sarmi position with the United States seizure of nearby Wakde Island. Later in this operation the 163d RCT was reinforced by elements of the 6th and 31st Infantry Divisions. Remnants of the Jap garrison from Arara withdrew overland to the west, over swamp and untraversed jungle ranges, across country believed to be inhabited by headhunters.

An Ordnance team composed of Major Marion Penn and Sgt John Lischalk left Hollandia on 17 June 1944 to stage with the 31st Infantry Division which was going to relieve the 6th Division at Sarmi. During the staging period the team assisted in training combat personnel for the coming operation. They left then with the first part of the Division, arriving at Sarmi on 12 July.

Contact was made with the 6th Division G-2, where it was found the CIC had shipped out considerable Japanese Ordnance equipment. The remaining equipment was turned over to Major Penn for packing and shipping.

Three days later a second Ordnance team, Lt Bishop and T/4 Winn, reported at Sarmi. They were attached to the 6th Division. Another Ordnance team, 1st Lt Nowakowski and T/4 Raymond Levy also reported in to 6th Division from Headquarters USASOS four days later. Lt Bishop's team pulled out for the Sansapor operation shortly after Lt Nowakowski's arrival.

Major Penn, having been ordered to the United States on rotation, was replaced in August by Capt Sternal who took this as his first assignment in the field as a Technical Intelligence officer. His team cooperated with Lt Nowakowski and T/4 Levy and continued to recover Japanese equipment, most of which was forwarded to the United States Army Technical Intelligence Depot at Finschhafen. Lt Nowakowski and T/4 Levy, when they had completed their mission in August, returned to the Ordnance analysis section, which was still at Brisbane and accompanied the section when it was shipped to Finschhafen.

HISTORY OF TECHNICAL INTELLIGENCE

Lt Overholt, who had been the Signal Technical Intelligence representative in the area left with the 6th Division to go on the Sansapor operation. Lt Daniels, Signal Corps, joined the 31st Division to carry on. All available information pertaining to this area was turned over to him. He continued collecting equipment and shipping it back to the Depot, at Finschhafen, until he was relieved of temporary duty with the 31st Infantry Division in September.

Biak: 27 May -- 20 Aug 44

On 27 May 1944 United States ground forces landed on Biak Island (Map Incl 12) which dominates the northern approaches to Geelvink Bay. The seizure of this island marked the practical end of the New Guinea campaign. Biak's capture, however, was not something to be written off the books in a few days. Within twenty-four hours after landing, it was clear that advance to the three airfields would not be easy.

The dominant factor of the operation was the high combat efficiency of the enemy. The 41st Infantry Division (minus 163d RCT) carried the early operation at Biak. United States ground forces held the initiative but it required some of the fiercest fighting in the history of Pacific warfare.

After a two-day battle ending 2 June, United States infantrymen won the commanding height called Mokmer Ridge; after a three hour battle on 3 June, they still held it; and by 16 June they had captured Mokmer Airdrome in a surprise flank movement to the enemy's rear.

The Biak Island operation was over except for mopping up, by 25 June after United States forces, in a sustained movement of envelopment, had broken stubborn Jap resistance to seize the other two airstrips, Borokoe and Sorido, and the port facilities of Sorido Village.

Lt Rowe, SC, on his own initiative had made arrangements to accompany the 41st Division on this operation. Having completed his mission at Hollandia, he departed from that base with the Division 23 May as commanding officer of the Signal Intelligence Team, and landed at Biak on H plus 50 minutes 27 May.

He operated closely with the task force Signal company, for it was found that this was the most satisfactory arrangement as they provided him with transportation and necessary personnel to recover the equipment from the field (this was before 5250th supervised the equipping of all teams). A place in the Signal depot was set aside for the storage of equipment and the Division Signal company extended every effort to facilitate the recovery and return of enemy equipment.

The activities of Lt Rowe were also closely coordinated with the Division G-2 and the Counter Intelligence Corps team. Both gave valuable assistance in reporting Signal dumps and aiding in their removal. (It was noticeable from operation to operation that the desire to help of the officers in charge of troops had a great deal to do with the success of the Technical Intelligence mission.)

There were no large fixed radio stations at Biak such as were found at Hollandia. There was one smaller station, however, located in the entrance to one of the large caves, but by the time this cave was cleared of Japs by using gasoline, bombs, and rockets, the sets were burned beyond recognition.

There was no evidence of the Japanese attempting to destroy any of their equipment either at operating positions or in dumps. None of the equipment recovered had been booby-trapped although the Japanese had had sufficient time to trap or destroy the equipment in the vicinity of the air strips. It was often found impossible, however, especially in the first few days of operation, to get all the equipment removed from the dumps as fast as they were reported or located, so "Off Limits" signs were posted to help prevent the looting of dumps before items of Intelligence value could be removed.

Lt Rowe remained at Biak until 3 July, when he returned to Base F (Finschhafen) with all of the Signal equipment captured -- approximately 4,500 pounds.

Lt Bishop and T/4 Winn were the first Ordnance Team to be sent into the Biak operation; they arrived early in July. However, before the fighting was completed, they were ordered by the Sixth Army to report to the 6th Division in the Maffin Bay area, where the Division was being relieved from the Arara -- Wakde -- Sarmi operation for the Sansapor operation. Considerable heavy Ordnance material they had collected on Biak had to be turned over to the task force Ordnance officer who shipped the equipment for them by water to Major Madigan at Hollandia. It arrived in good condition.

Lt Claude F. Pope, Pvt Albert L. Morath, Pvt Richard E. Reynolds (all newly assigned to 5250th), composing Ordnance Team No. 1, were sent to Biak during September to take over after Lt Bishop and T/4 Winn had left to join the 6th Division. A considerable quantity of enemy Ordnance materiel was still available and was shipped by them to the Depot at Finschhafen.

On 28 September Ordnance Team No. 1 proceeded to 24th Division, at that time staging for the coming Philippine Islands operation. Because of orders, for this movement, this Ordnance team also was unable to remain at Biak until all the captured materiel had been shipped, but arrangements were made with S-4, Headquarters Base "H" (Biak), to ship it to the Technical Intelligence Depot at Finschhafen.

Engineer Team No. 3, Captain Connors, S/Sgt Smith and T/4 Sherwood, arrived at Biak from the Hollandia operation 10 June. They had taken off, like Lt Rowe, on their own initiative -- hopped a plane ride when they heard that considerable enemy Engineer equipment was being captured in that area.

Early in the Pacific War, Technical Intelligence teams operated under General Orders from Army Headquarters. They planned their own itinerary, secured transportation, took over enemy equipment from combat troops to whom they were not necessarily attached, and did all this by a rather comprehensive authority from the Army that they were "to proceed wherever necessary to secure captured enemy equipment". They often had to win the cooperation of men who had never heard of Technical Intelligence and had no conception of its mission. They not only had to be combat men, technical analysists, and Army scroungers of the first order, but also first class salesmen. They talked their way through.

Although the Biak operation had been declared "practically won" by various news commentators in the States, the hardest fighting was still to come. When Captain Connors and his team arrived, United States troops still had only an unsteady hold on the original beachhead -- the Japs took the beach road away several times a week.

The general procedure for Technical Intelligence teams, at that time, was to recover the equipment, submit a report, assemble all equipment at one point, and then turn it over to

the base transportation officer. It was found more and more
desirable, as the war proceeded, for the teams to safehand
equipment back to the Depot to insure its arrival intact.
Engineer Team No. 3, however, like the other two teams, had
to leave Biak before the equipment -- an entire Japanese
machine shop, mines, water purifier unit, etc -- could be
shipped to the Depot at Finschhafen. Capt Connors, therefore, crated the material and left it with the task force
Engineers.

The team left Biak early in July and Capt Creed called
Major Harwood's Engineer Team (T/3 Ellyett and T/3 Paris) to
go up to Biak from Finschhafen to finish collecting the equipment and to return that on hand to the Depot. Major Harwood,
who had been assigned to the 5250th Technical Intelligence
Company in June along with Capt Connors, and who had the only
other Engineer Technical Intelligence team in the Theater,
arrived at Biak in September after the close of operations
(20 August). This time arrangements had been made through
the 5250th for the team to be vested with more specific
authority to take over equipment from troops in the area.

During this post operational period, the following
additional teams, all personnel new in the field, arrived at
Biak:

C.W.S.

2d Lt Allen Phillips   Pvt Robert Dennigan
T/5 J. L. Garner

Medical

2d Lt Earl Raab

Quartermaster

Capt Joseph Mulvey   Pvt Charles Wright
Pvt Leon Myers

Signal

2d Lt Henry Jarvis   T/3 John Lotz

These teams not only recovered equipment remaining in the Biak area, but also gained experience in Technical Intelligence work under field conditions as preliminary training for combat duty during the coming Philippine campaign. Late in September the following teams received orders to report to Hollandia to stage with the 24th Infantry Division for the Philippines: Lt Phillip's CWS Team; Lt Raab of the Medical Corps; Capt Mulvey's Quartermaster Team; and Lt Jarvis' Signal Team.

A Technical Intelligence Coordinator is Appointed to Sixth Army

At the beginning of the war, Technical Intelligence had been dependent upon concurrence of the Army before they could go into any operation; the Army could refuse, or having granted permission, could change its mind.

Upon the formation of USAFFE another link was added, and the request to go into combat had to be sent to them. They in turn requested permission from the Army.

Even once having gained permission, all was not smooth sailing. The teams frequently would arrive at the Division or Corps for staging, only to discover that the Task Force had not been notified that the Technical Intelligence teams were to be attached to their headquarters. Not knowing anything about it, the Corps would sometimes order them back or simply pick up and go off on operations, leaving the teams. This is what had happened in connection with the Cape Gloucester operation when a specially formed unit, sent up for staging after permission had originally been given by the Army, was denied permission to go on the operation.

Late in June 1944 Col N. B. Sauve forwarded a letter to Sixth Army, outlining a plan for a Technical Intelligence officer to be attached to Sixth Army to supervise training programs and to coordinate the activities of Technical Intelligence personnel supplied by USASOS to Sixth Army. Sixth Army agreed.

Authorization was then obtained from USAFFE for direct communication between Sixth Army and USASOS on Technical Intelligence matters (thus skipping the USAFFE link), and authority was granted for USASOS to issue orders attaching Technical Intelligence personnel to Sixth Army.

Captain Creed had arrived in the Theater during June and had been placed on detached service with the 5250th. He and T/3 Peterson were placed at first on temporary duty to Headquarters Alamo Force to instruct the 112th and 158th Cavalry Regimental Combat Teams, which were to participate in the Woodlark and Kiriwina Islands operations, in the identification and operation of enemy Ordnance equipment.

The first week of July 1944, Capt Creed was placed on detached service with the Sixth Army as the first Coordinator of Technical Intelligence for an Army in this Theater. Attached to the Office of the Assistant Chief of Staff, G-2, Sixth Army, his work was to coordinate activities of all Technical Intelligence units placed on temporary duty with the Army; to maintain liaison between the AC of S, G-2, Sixth Army and the AC of S, G-2, USASOS; to advise G-2, USASOS, as to the number and composition of Technical Intelligence units required by the Army; to coordinate the activities of Sixth Army's Technical Intelligence units; to supervise the training program for troops on Technical Intelligence matters; and to act as liaison officer with the United States Army Technical Intelligence Depot.

T/3 John Lotz was assigned to G-2, Sixth Army, to handle the clerical work, and Capt Sternal and T/Sgt Peterson were attached to the Army to assist Capt Creed in conducting a training program on the use of Japanese weapons.

Altogether, the efficiency of the set-up was improved one hundred percent. Early in September Capt Creed came down from Sixth Army for a conference with Col Sauve' on the number and composition of teams for future operations, and arrangements were made to supply the requisite personnel. Task Forces then knew ahead of time what Technical Intelligence teams to expect and how their work was to be coordinated with the plans of the Division or Corps. Preliminary arrangements were also made for the Technical Intelligence teams to assist in the pre-combat training program. As it turned out, closer coordination was established between the teams and key personnel at Task Force headquarters as well as with the troops, and the flow of information and materiel between the teams in the field and the Depot was considerably expedited.

The Depot at Finschhafen Is Enlarged

In mid-July Major Oakle Bullock, Corps of Engineers, from South Pacific Area, and two enlisted men, were transferred to the 5250th Technical Intelligence Company, and after a few days orientation, were transferred to Finschhafen to process equipment sent in by the two Engineer teams -- Major Harwood's and Capt Connor's -- sent out into the field. By this time all captured enemy equipment was being forwarded to Finschhafen rather than to Brisbane for analysis and trans-shipment to the United States.

Lt Col Jones, Engineer Intelligence Officer from USASOS, was sent from Brisbane to Finschhafen and Hollandia to study the facilities of the new Depot, to make disposition of captured Engineer equipment, to confer with the new Engineer Intelligence teams and the newly appointed Sixth Army liaison officer, Capt Creed.

In August Captain Gordon Boss, who was interested in and had knowledge of Japanese equipment, requested transfer to the 5250th. Pending assignment to a field team, he was detailed to the Ordnance section to relieve Capt Birleffi, who was being transferred to the Office of the Assistant Chief of Staff, G-2, USASOS. During the first week of September, Major Andrew M. Neff and three enlisted men, comprising CWS Team No. 8 (team numbers, in some cases from here on, until they were re-designated by 5250th for the Army of Occupation for Japan a year later, were designated by the War Department and did not follow in chronological order those already assigned in this Theater) left Brisbane on temporary duty with the Depot at Base F.

An United States Navy Mobile Explosives Investigation Unit (MEIU) composed of one officer and one enlisted man, was attached to the United States Army Technical Intelligence Depot at Base "F" at about the same time. The orders as written for this personnel permitted them to accompany the Technical Intelligence teams in the field with the Sixth Army.

It was decided that all Technical Intelligence teams for Sixth and Eighth Armies would stage at the Technical Intelligence Depot at Finschhafen and that therefore the housing facilities would need to be expanded so that personnel might train, and

analytical work might still be carried on during the staging
period. It was contemplated, by then that more than one hundred Technical Intelligence officers and enlisted men would
be **stationed** at the Technical Intelligence Depot at one time.

On 29 July, the United States Army Technical Intelligence
Depot moved to a new location situated four miles north of
Headquarters Base "F", on North 21st Street. The new location
of the Depot covered a five acre area, and contained six large
buildings, each approximately 100 feet long, 20 feet wide and
15 feet high, capable of accomodating one of the services'
depot and laboratory comfortably within its own structure.
The site for the Depot was selected by Major Johnston, Major
McKoy and Captain Creed. Captain Creed had arrived on 23
July, bringing with him a large shipment of enemy equipment
from Sixth Army.

The Chemical Warfare, Engineer, Medical, Quartermaster,
and Signal analysis laboratories, having completed shipments
of all materiel pertaining to their sections that had accumulated at Brisbane, arrived at Finschhafen on 25 July. The
Ordnance Intelligence Section was delayed in moving until
materiel on hand had been shipped to the United States, but
by the end of August was established with the other sections
at Finschhafen with Lt Cameron who had been sent forward with
three officers and six enlisted men to Finschhafen in charge.
The building frames and roof had been erected with the help
of a labor detail from the Base. The floor was laid, but
there were no sides, partitions or fencing when the analysis
sections arrived from Brisbane. Everyone assisted in com-
pleting construction, fencing and protection of the buildings
and in the installation of sanitation, lighting and piping
equipment. (Water was supplied from a nearby 70 foot water-
fall). When completed the new United States Army Technical
Intelligence Depot contained facilities for the analysis laboratories as well as for quarters for Technical Intelligence
personnel at the Depot and from the field.

Sansapor: 30 Jul -- 31 Aug 1944

The Allies leapfrogged again to Sansapor (Map Incl 12).
Immediate strategic gain was to isolate another 15,000 Japanese troops and to push the United States offensive front
200 miles closer to the Philippines.

47

Middelburg and Amsterdam Islands and the adjacent shore-
line known as Sansapor were seized by American amphibious
forces on 30 July with virtually no opposition. Elements of
the 6th Infantry Division directed operations, and although
destroyers, cruisers, and RAAF Kittyhawks were on hand to
provide sea and air cover, no preliminary bombardment was
necessary. All objectives were occupied by mid-morning.

The occupation of Sansapor concluded Allied re-occupa-
tion of strategic centers along the northern coast of Dutch
New Guinea and established Allied air bases from Milne Bay
along the entire coast of New Guinea. The enemy was no
longer able to operate either by air or sea beyond the Hal-
mahera-Philippine line, which was the main defense cover
for his conquered empire in the Southwest Pacific.

Rather than organize for an attack against American
forces at Sansapor, the Japanese Second Army withdrew in
barges and by overland trails toward the south and west.
The retreat was general from all the one-time Japanese strongholds in Geelvink Bay and in upper Vogelkop. (Map Incl 12)
A quick end had been put to the effectiveness of the Japanese Army which was charged with the defense of the entire
territory.

The Ordnance Team composed of Lt Bishop and T/4 Winn,
who had recently been recalled from the Biak operation,
loaded out of Maffin Bay with the 6th Division and landed
in the Sansapor operation on D-Day, 30 July 1944. Reconnaissance of the immediate area showed no signs of any Ordnance materiel and upon writing for reports from the infantry patrols, still no materiel was recovered. The unit
then proceeded back to Sixth Army Headquarters VOCG, and
received orders to return to Headquarters USASOS, which had
by this time moved up to Hollandia. The unit reported there
on 10 August 1944.

Chemical Warfare Service Team No. 6 (Lt Phillips, T/5
Garner and Pfc Dennigan) and Lt Jacob Overholt, Signal Technical Intelligence representative, staged with 6th Division
at Maffin Bay with a CIC Team. Lt Overholt located a quantity of enemy equipment of Intelligence value, and returned
from Sansapor operations 20 August. The Division G-2 and the
CIC Team were co-operative and the Division Ordnance officer
was very helpful in organizing patrols to search for equipment on this mission. Officers and enlisted men of the
Dutch Army assisted on patrols and it was found that their
method of operation and experience were very instructive.

On a small surprise operation such as this where there
were few troops to oppose the Allied landing, usually there
was comparatively little enemy equipment recovered of Intelligence value.

The following lessons, incidental, but typical and rather
interesting, were learned on this operation: transportation
should be amphibious in forward areas of New Guinea for the
Technical Intelligence work; officers and enlisted men should
be equipped with side-arms as well as carbines or sub-machine
guns because the larger weapons had to be laid aside to examine or handle equipment found in enemy dumps; captured
equipment should be sent back by messenger without having it
delayed by CIC at intermediate bases;

For best cooperation in the Division, everything found
should be reported to the Division Service officers (Ordnance,
Signal, etc.) and the various units of the Division contacted
through them; recovered searchlights should be turned over
to the Division for use on the perimeter, for by lighting
up the perimeter, unnecessary firing and uneasiness would be
brought to a minimum.

To encourage cooperation in turn, any equipment found,
other than that pertaining to the individual team, should
be turned over to the proper officer; enemy command posts
reported to G-2 should be be investigated -- valuable equipment could often be found in the vicinity; in case a dump
for one service were found, the vicinity should be scouted
for approximately 100 yards -- dumps for other services
could often be located nearby; dumps were usually found
within 50 yards of a vehicle trail or road.

Acquaintance of natives in the area should be made,
for they would bring information concerning the location of
dumps and though this information would be given to G-2,
very often a day or two could be saved by getting it direct;

Officers and enlisted men should receive a refresher
course in scouting and patroling adaptive to the Theater,
including particular instructions in organizing and directing search patrols.

HISTORY OF TECHNICAL INTELLIGENCE

Tempo of Activity for Technical Intelligence Increases

During the late summer and early fall of 1944 additional personnel were procured and changes of assignment were made for the 5250th Technical Intelligence Composite Company, Separate (Provisional). On 25 August Major Manley who had recently been promoted, was officially appointed Commanding Officer of the 5250th and Coordinator of Technical Intelligence Office of the AC of S, G-2, USASOS. He relieved Major Johnston, who turned his full attention to directing Ordnance Intelligence for the coming Philippine Islands campaign. 1st Lt Birleffi was designated Assistant Coordinator and Assistant Company Commander; Lt Van Slyck was appointed Administrative Officer for the 5250th for all matters pertaining to Technical Intelligence with the Technical Intelligence Depot, under the general supervision of the Assistant Executive, S-2, Base F and under the direction of Headquarters USASOS.

Lt Cameron, scheduled for assignment to a field team with Eighth Army, was replaced as officer in charge of the Ordnance analysis section by Major Madigan; Capt Lawrence A. Sternal and 1st Lt Phillip Kurzel requested and were assigned to the 5250th in Ordnance Intelligence; T/4 William L. Whittington, T/4 Ralph J. Pickerell, T/5 William R. Holland, T/5 John M. Rosanett, Pvt Clinton A. Bagwell, Pvt Haywood L. Henderson, and Pvt Misco S. Moore were detailed for duty with the Depot. T/5 Richard T. McAlpin, who reported to the Depot from the USASOS G-2 Office, took over a great deal of the administrative-clerical work.

The policy was continued of having personnel not on duty with the administrative section and field teams assigned to the analysis section, pending request for personnel by Sixth and Eighth Armies. Upon request, personnel were attached to the Armies for assignment as field teams to task forces.

The number of personnel assigned to the 5250th for Technical Intelligence duties as of 31 August 1944 was: Sixteen officers and twenty-five enlisted men on temporary duty from the War Department; thirty officers and thirty enlisted men assigned from this Theater; total: 44 officers and 55 enlisted men.

HISTORY OF TECHNICAL INTELLIGENCE

Late in September, Major Manley submitted a check sheet to G-4, USASOS, requesting that necessary directives be issued transferring the Headquarters of 5250th from APO 501 to APO 707. At this time, Col Sauve', accompanied by the G-2 Intermediate Section, departed from Brisbane to Finschhafen to inspect the Depot there, to confer with the Base S-2, and to witness a firing demonstration of Japanese weapons.

The dissemination of written information on Technical Intelligence was constantly going on: A notebook on Japanese Chemical Warfare was distributed in September, and the first number of the Chemical Warfare Intelligence Digest also went to press. This digest, which publicized up to date Chemical Warfare Intelligence information as it was received, and generalized descriptions of captured Chemical Warfare materiel, provided pertinent information until it could be consolidated in more permanent form in the Japanese Chemical Warfare notebook. An extensive report on Jap munition markings was published in November and December 1944. This report was the result of almost two years' research through captured enemy documents, munitions and reports from other theaters. Its primary function was to serve as a guide in distinguishing Japanese Chemical Warfare Munitions from Japanese regular munitions.

In September, USAFFE published Circular No. 83 (Incl 15) a standard operating procedure recommended by Major Manley to clarify methods of disposition of captured enemy equipment and documents. This circular set forth the responsibilities of troop commanders in collecting, safe guarding and turning over captured materiel and established a control policy in regard to souveniring. As a result of the clarification of both these phases of Technical Intelligence, coordination between troop commanders and Technical Intelligence units was considerably expedited.

The last operation for Technical Intelligence in the southern islands would be Morotai. Looking ahead from there plans were already being made for the next move of the United States Army Technical Intelligence Depot -- this time to the Philippines. Manila was selected as the next site, and it was decided that the Depot this time would be moved as a unit, rather than by sections.

Morotai: 15 Sep -- 4 Oct 1944

The Allies moved into position for the drive on the
Philippines when the 31st and 32d Infantry Divisions under
command of XI Corps seized Morotai, northernmost of the Halmahera Islands, Netherlands East Indies (Map Incl 12), and
marines and infantrymen from the Central Pacific struck 500
miles to the northeast to invade Palau.

Beautifully coordinated, both landings occurred on the
morning of 15 September 1944. On Morotai, all objectives
had been seized by H plus four hours. On Palau, the resistance
was as tough as American troops had come up against.

In taking Morotai, which lies some 315 miles northwest
of Sansapor, New Guinea, and 300 miles southeast of Mindanao,
Philippine Islands, United States troops capitalized on the
element of surprise. Heavy air bombardment during the preceeding weeks had deceived the enemy into concentrating most
of his strength along the coastal flats of Kaoe Bay in northern Halmahera. Morotai, dominating the approaches to this
Bay, was but lightly defended, and what few Japs were
garrisoned there retreated into the hills during the preliminary naval bombardment. Casualties to United States
ground forces were extremely light and there were no air and
sea losses.

Technical Intelligence Unit No. 1 (personnel present on
this operation are listed in Incl 3) left for Aitape on 28
August 1944 for temporary duty with XI Corps to stage for the
15 September Trade Winds operation at Morotai. The Unit,
with Capt Everrett C. Lary in command, left Aitape on 9 September and landed with the fourth wave at Morotai. Captain
Connor's Engineer Team No. 3 (S/Sgt Smith, T/4 Sherwood)
found little enemy Engineer equipment on this operation but
did obtain information on Japanese Engineering standards and
fortifications.

On 11 September Capt Connors was assigned to Headquarters,
USASOS, as Engineer Technical Intelligence Officer Rear Echelon
Services of Supply.

Lt William E. Winterstein, who had just recently report-
ed to the 5250th, T/Sgt Eugence F. Rossi, and Pvt Nick
Vannucci, were assigned as the Ordnance Intelligence Team at
Morotai, also reported no new items recovered, and returned in
October to the Technical Intelligence Depot at Finschhafen.

HISTORY OF TECHNICAL INTELLIGENCE

Morotai had turned out to be one of those Cook's Tours.
No new equipment from the operation was reported and nothing
whatsoever was shipped to the United States Army Technical
Intelligence Depot at Base F. It was the sort of unproductive
operation from an Intelligence stand point that was so in-
comprehensible to Washington, yet -- there simply was no
equipment of Intelligence value to send back.

C H A P T E R   V

RETURN TO THE PHILIPPINES

October -- December 1944

By October 1944, by means of island hopping, the United States Forces were ready to embark on the Philippine campaign. By this time, knocking out pillboxes and isolated strong points had been developed into a science, the science of fighting a new type of warfare. Storming the beaches was also far from new, for behind the doughfeet lay such campaigns as Buna, Lae, Hollandia, Biak and many others. Some had been bloody and discouraging but a big job had been completed with exceedingly meager resources. With the Philippines (Map Incl 16) in sight, the picture was completely changed. This time the United States Army had the men and the materiel, as well as the determination to carry the war through to a successful conclusion.

The 13th of October 1944 saw a gigantic two-pronged convoy of 600 transports, landing craft and warships moving northward from Hollandia and westward from the Admiralties. Aboard were troops of the Sixth Army, the X and XXIV Corps. The group was escorted by air and sea by units of the Far East Air Force and the RAAF and elements of the United States Third and Seventh Fleets. General MacArthur was in personal command of the armada that was to make good the promise, "I shall return".

On 17 October, the 6th Ranger Battalion struck the opening blow when they seized two islets guarding the entrance to Leyte Gulf (Map, Incl 16 & 17) and on the morning of 20 October, unloading began on four beachheads along Leyte's east coast.

Before the finish of the operation, enemy forces on the island had risen to 150,000, including reinforcements brought in from the other islands. However, the initial attack was so overwhelming that Tacloban, Leyte, (Map, Incl 17) was captured with a loss of less than a dozen men and in less than two weeks the United States forces held two-thirds of the island of Leyte.

HISTORY OF TECHNICAL INTELLIGENCE

Landing Operations and Enemy Tactics

On the morning of 20 October at 0600 hours, the naval bombardment of Leyte began. From 0600 hours until 0900 hours the battleships and cruisers fired approximately 2600 tons of explosives on that island. At 0900 hours, while the heavy units still continued their bombardment, the rocket launching LCI's moved up for the final blow before the actual assault troops began landing. They went in abreast of each other in a long line toward the beach, and began launching their rockets. From 0900 till 1000 hours all that could be heard was one long continuous rumbling roar coming from the island. By this time the first assault wave had almost reached the beach, the LCI's ceased their fire, and the first wave landed on Leyte against only slight opposition. The initial landings were made by the 7th and 24th Infantry Division, and the 1st Cavalry Divisions.

There was no doubt of the sincerity of the natives. They were overjoyed at their release. There were, inevitably, a few pro-Japanese natives who acted as spies for the enemy. With the exception of the children the natives were in poor physical condition, having suffered from malnutrition. Clothing and household effects were virtually non-existent as the Japanese had requisitioned or commandeered almost every item. Families had been turned out of their homes to make room for the billeting of the Japs.

Operation of Technical Intelligence on Leyte

It was the plan for the Leyte operation to have three Technical Intelligence field units with the combat troops. They were organized along the lines of the first composite unit that participated in the Hollandia operation. Each unit was attached to a division and was composed of teams of all -- or nearly all -- of the services. Complete coverage of the designated combat sector, and coordination in administration and operation were thus assured.

Late in September, Technical Intelligence Unit No. 1 was placed on temporary duty with the 24th Infantry Division at Hollandia to stage for the Leyte operation. This Unit was composed of the following personnel:

Engineer Team No. 4

Major Kenneth C. Harwood   T/3 Elsworth P. Paris
T/3 James W. Ellyett, Jr.

Ordnance Team No. 1

1st Lt Claude F. Pope   Pvt Richard E. Reynolds
Pfc Albert L. Moruth

Signal Team

2d Lt Henry Jarvis   T/3 John L. Lotz

Leyte was the first operation for the Signal Team, composed
of personnel recently assigned to the 5250th. Major Harwood's
team which was to operate as part of the advance base depot
team, and Lt Pope's team, had gained some experience in the
field during the post-operations period at Biak, but it was
their first combat assignment with Technical Intelligence.
Capt Joseph A. Mulvey, who had been assigned as quartermaster
Intelligence officer for this Unit, was delayed and did not
arrive at the embarkation point in time for the operation.

During staging, members of Technical Intelligence Unit
No. 1 met with the AC of S, G-2, of the Division, to whom they
were attached with members of ATIS, METU No. 1, and the CIC
team. A complete briefing, methods of working together, priority in the collection of enemy equipment, etc., were thoroughly covered. As METU had the best facilities for rapid dissemination to the combat troops, it was decided that they would get
first call on all explosive materiel captured. The Technical
Intelligence Ordnance Team would get next highest priority.

Plans were made for the Unit to go ashore in the second wave.
It became a standard policy throughout the rest of the war for
Technical Intelligence teams to go in early -- within one hour
if possible -- after the first wave landed, to prevent troops
from souveniring valuable equipment, thus destroying its use-
fulness for Technical Intelligence.

During staging, the Unit checked team and individual equip-
ment, and drew replacements for shortages. At 1800 hours, 13
October, the Unit sailed with the convoy from Hollandia to
Leyte.

During landing operations, Major Harwood's two enlisted men, T/? Ellyott and Morris, distinguished themselves on Red Beach by recovering an abandoned D-7 Bulldozer and unloading it while under enemy fire.

Technical Intelligence Unit No. 1 covered Leyte Valley on this operation, but as little equipment was captured, it was decided that they should return to the United States Army Technical Intelligence Depot at Finschhafen after only eight days in the field. They took back with them the equipment that had been recovered.

Technical Intelligence Unit No. 2 which was attached to the 1st Cavalry Division for the Leyte operation, was composed of the following teams:

Chemical Warfare Service Team No. 7

Captain Everett C. Lary   T/Sgt Julius L. Horton

Medical Section Team No. 4

Captain Norris Able

Quartermaster Section

Captain Robert S. Gunderson   S/Sgt William J. Poss
T/Sgt Eugene F. Rossi

Signal Section

1st Lt William F. Howind   T/Sgt Robert J. McConkie

Ordnance Team No. 11

Captain Laurence A. Sternal   Pvt Robert De Freitas
T/Sgt Paul F. Quick

Engineer Team No. 2

Captain Donald C. Connors   T/4 Roger E. Sherwood

Most of this personnel, with the exception of Capt Connors' team which had been at Hollandia and Biak, were new to Technical Intelligence and had only a short period of training in the Analysis sections of the United States Army Technical Intelligence Depot.

After drawing their vehicles (which had to be sent up later) and other equipment at Hollandia, the teams proceeded to Manus Island, in the Admiralties, to stage with the 1st Cavalry Division for Leyte.

Technical Intelligence Unit No. 2 operated in Northern Leyte and after the departure of Technical Intelligence Unit No. 1 also operated in the 24th Infantry Division Sector in the Leyte Valley.

Capt Sternal was appointed Acting Coordinator of Technical Intelligence with the Sixth Army in addition to his duties as an Ordnance Technical Intelligence officer. He temporarily replaced Capt Creel who had received a serious head wound from shrapnel during operations. As Acting Co-ordinator for Sixth Army Capt Sternal evaluated and compiled reports submitted by the other Technical Intelligence teams and collaborated with the other specialists for dissemination of information (particularly on new equipment's G-2 publication to combat units. The presence of a Technical Intelligence coordinator at an advance Army Headquarters proved to be of great help during the course of the operation -- questions directed to Capt Sternal concerning Japanese equipment, particularly Ordnance, were innumerable.

Technical Intelligence Unit No. 2 had not been attached to the 1st Cavalry until 30 September, a little over a week before the Division sailed and too late to enable jeeps and trailers to be shipped with the Unit; the absence of authorized transportation severely handicapped team operations and Capt Norris Able, Medical Officer, had to be detained to accompany a rear detachment to bring in additional vehicles.

By 1 November Technical Intelligence Unit No. 2 as well as No. 1 had completed its mission and had boarded a ship for return to the United States Army Technical Intelligence Depot at Finschhafen.

The following teams composed Technical Intelligence Unit No. 3:

CWS Intelligence Team No. 5

2d Lt Victor Del Guercio   Pfc Edgar Mulligan
T/5 Gaspare Mangiaricina

Engineer Intelligence Team No. 5

Capt Gardner O. Johnson
T/5 William C. Garrett

Pvt Henry Carson

Medical Intelligence Team No. 1

Captain Raymond F. Galloway

Medical Intelligence Team No. 4

Captain Morris Able

Ordnance Intelligence Team No. 2

Captain Gordon Bess

T/Sgt Glenn E. Peterson

Ordnance Intelligence Team No. 4

Captain Edward Nowakowski

T/Sgt Paul F. Quick

Quartermaster Intelligence Team No. 4

Major Sidney K. Pope

Signal Intelligence Team No. 2

2d Lt Jacob H. Overholt

T/4 Robert S. Traub

Technical Intelligence Unit No. 3 was placed on temporary duty with Army Service Command and on further temporary duty to Headquarters, Base K, Tacloban, Leyte where they arrived on D plus one. A permanent base was organized here from which trips to all parts of the island were made.

Technical Intelligence Unit No. 3 at first functioned primarily as a provisional depot unit to receive and make shipments of captured enemy equipment brought in by Technical Intelligence Units 1 and 2 operating with the combat troops in the forward areas.

During the first ten days after arrival, Technical Intelligence Unit No. 3 was engaged in preparing the field Depot for the receiving and shipping of the incoming captured equipment. This was a temporary advance depot similar

to that at Hollandia. Except for certain bulky equipment
shipped directly to the United States, most of the captured
materiel was trans-shipped to the United States Army Technical
Intelligence Depot at Finschhafen for further analysis. Part
of the time was also spent in checking the ammunition dumps
in the vicinity of Tacloban and Palo. A short time later
when both Technical Intelligence Units No. 1 and No. 2 had
been withdrawn from the operation, Unit No. 3 was left as the
only Technical Intelligence unit on Leyte island. As such,
this Unit had the dual responsibility of running the depot and
keeping contact with all combat organizations engaged in this
operation.

On the same day Technical Intelligence Unit No. 2 departed from Leyte, Ordnance Team No. 4, composed of Capt Edward
Nowakowski and T/Sgt Quick arrived. This team, which was
originally assigned to Field Unit No. 2 had had to return to
the Technical Intelligence Depot at Finschhafen because of
some confusion in shipping arrangements and had taken a later
ship. They reported to 1st Cavalry upon arrival, but were
relieved from that organization a week later and placed on
temporary duty with Army Service Command.

Since Technical Intelligence Units 1 and 2 had left, Capt
Nowakowski and T/Sgt Quick functioned with Technical Intelligence
Unit No. 3 at the depot and aided in collecting materiel.

After completely covering the area in the vicinity of the
depot, this team and Technical Intelligence Unit No. 3 went
into the field with the 24th Infantry Division, covering the
whole front of the Leyte campaign. Much equipment and materiel
was recovered during this drive and field reports on many new
items were prepared.

Considerable equipment was recovered after the Japanese
reinforcement paratrooper attack near San Pablo and in the Ormoc
area in the 7th and 77th Infantry Divisions' sectors. However,
the lack of time, the large area involved, and the rugged
terrain features, prevented the evacuation of large quantities
of the materiel captured.

Besides maintaining liaison with the previously mentioned
units, liaison was also maintained with the 1st Cavalry, the
11th Airborne Division and the 24th, 32d and 96th Infantry
Divisions. If any outstanding recoveries of enemy equipment
were made by these organizations, trained Technical Intelligence personnel were made available to handle the field analysis of the equipment.

There were no shipments of enemy equipment from the field depot at Leyte until towards the end of November since routing to Finschhafen had been stopped and no ships left for the United States until then.

Technical Intelligence for the Leyte operation as a whole was not as productive of captured enemy equipment as had been anticipated. It had been assumed that large stores of enemy equipment would be uncovered there, but that assumption proved to be false. Due primarily to terrain and weather conditions, the type of fighting encountered on Leyte throughout nearly all of the early phases of the operation was spasmodic. Few enemy dumps were captured and proportionately, the quantities of equipment recovered intact were limited. Upon the completion of the Leyte operation, four new Technical Intelligence Units, 4, 5, 6 and 7, were formed for the "M" operation. (Personnel of these units are shown in Incl 3) All three Technical Intelligence Units were disbanded and the personnel used as a nuclei of experienced men for the new teams which were to be formed.

During December Engineer Intelligence Team No. 7 (Lt John F. Keane, Pvt James W. Stephens, Pvt Christopher W. Tamer) of the re-organized Technical Intelligence Unit No. 1 engaged in collecting specimens of all available captured enemy Engineer equipment from the Sixth Army Engineer teams in the field with a view to setting up a training program for Eighth Army Engineer units. Special attention was given to land mines, booby traps and demolitions. On 28 December the training materiel was turned over to the Engineer Section, Headquarters, Eighth Army.

Operations on Leyte Are Turned Over To Eighth Army

As the control of all operations on Leyte was to be turned over to Eighth Army, Lt Col Erle H. Julian who had been assigned to Eighth Army in late October as Technical Intelligence Coordinator and a reorganized Technical Intelligence Unit No. 1, joined that Headquarters on 14 November 1944. (Personnel composing the Unit are shown in Incl 3). As Eighth Army had not participated in any combat the time was spent by Technical Intelligence Unit No. 1 in making contacts with the X and XXIV Corps and with the associated service chiefs. Plans were made so that upon Eighth Army's taking command of the remainder of the Leyte operation, there would be no time lost in taking to the field. They were ordered to report to 38th Infantry Division on 26 December 1944, the same day Eighth Army took operational control.

HISTORY OF TECHNICAL INTELLIGENCE

A survey was made of all captured Ordnance equipment in western Leyte. Throughout this area large quantities of equipment were r covered. Eighteen light tanks, type 95, were destroyed in the mountains below Limon. As these tanks formed road blocks, they were shoved over the sides of the rugged mountain roads to dispose of them. Only two remained in a position such as would allow for their evacuation.

Ammunition was encountered in large quantities. However, as many of the dumps were practically located on the road, the Engineers destroyed them as a safety precaution as they cleared the roads for movement of military supplies. Enough ammunition of all types, never-the-less, remained in good condition to satisfy the requests for its use in analysis and test firing. A considerable quantity of renovated American ammunition was found in the captured dumps.

Japanese ammunition and materiel were used by United States troops wherever possible. Japanese 81 mm mortar ammunition, for instance, being utilized as harassing fire against the enemy.

The Japanese placed great emphasis on destroying United States artillery pieces. For this, suicide tactics were employed. A Jap soldier would strap an explosive charge to his body and charge into the field piece, destroying it and himself as he pulled the igniter detonating the charge. Similar tactics were used against tanks. Captured documents on anti-tank tactics described this procedure as a part of their training.

During the first half of January 1945 Ordnance Intelligence Team No. 6 (Capt Cameron, T/3 Carl R. Simmons, Pvt Nick Vannucci) was also assigned to the 38th Division, but as that division was not to be committed to combat for some time, arrangements were made for this team to again cover the combat areas of the 7th and 77th Divisions in western Leyte. These two divisions were engaged in mopping up activities at the time. Cooperation from XXIV Corps, in command in that area, was excellent in the evacuation of equipment. They supplied all the necessary trucks and labor to get the job done. The Technical Intelligence Ordnance enlisted men supervised the work, as a total of 65 tons of enemy materiel was evacuated and shipped to Base K, Tacloban, Leyte, for trans-shipment to the United States Army Technical Intelligence Depot at Finschhafen.

C H A P T E R VI

UNITED STATES ARMY TECHNICAL INTELLIGENCE DEPOT

October 1944 -- February 1945

The United States Army Technical Intelligence Depot was the nerve center for Technical Intelligence activities. It was administered directly under the control of G-2, USASOS, with each service operating an analysis section under the technical supervision of its respective service chief. Technical Intelligence units preparing for operation staged at the Depot and upon termination of duty in the field returned there, where the personnel were intergrated into the analysis section staff. All equipment and materiel recovered by the teams was brought or sent to the Technical Intelligence Depot for study and research.

Shipping from the Depot at Finschhafen to the United States improved considerably during October, November and December. Shipping from outlying bases was slow. A quantity of equipment particularly Signal Corps and Ordnance materiel was received from the New Guinea operations, Biak, Sansapor and Morotai, and as a result of the rapid advance of United States troops during January and February in Leyte, an unusually large quantity from all the services was recovered. At the same time a steady stream of small items confiscated by base censors and base Intelligence officers flowed in. Japanese aircraft equipment shipped from Aitape and other New Guinea bases was transshipped to Air Technical Intelligence, Far East Air Force, for disposition.

Some confusion in the handling of name plates was evident. The War Department had directed that all nameplates should be mailed to the Director of Intelligence, Army Service Forces, Washington, D. C., but the Chiefs of Services prohibited the removal of nameplates from equipment to be shipped to the United States. However, Technical and economic warfare Intelligence requirements could both be satisfied by double distribution of nameplate information and therefore, the following procedure went into effect: nameplates received from Technical Intelligence teams, Analysis Sections or postal censors, unless

cleared by the Allied Translator and Interpreter Section with
the task forces, were forwarded to the AC of S, G-2, Hq. USASOS,
from where they were air mailed to the Director of Intelligence,
Army Service Forces, Washington. Nameplates of extreme technical significance, integral parts of the equipment, were
photographed or duplicated by rubbings, and the prints, negatives or rubbings mailed to Army Service Forces, Washington.

Throughout this period nameplates and operating instruction panels were received regularly in quantity from Technical
Intelligence teams in the field and from postal consors. Preliminary translations were rendered for the benefit of the
analysis sections and the plates were then transmitted directly to the United States.

In view of comments from consignees in the United States,
packing and crating of equipment for shipment was conducted
with greater care for durability. Additional precautions
were taken to insure adequate labeling of crates and inclosing
of sufficient copies of vouchers and packing lists to facilitate recognition of equipment and acknowledgement of receipt.

Lt Stanger was relieved as Depot Officer for another
assignment 15 December 1944. On temporary duty with the Technical Intelligence Depot as Acting Property Officer and Assistant Administrative Officer were 2d Lts Edwin A. Kurtz and
Kenneth A. Kuykendall, Intelligence officers assigned to Base
"F".

The following Technical Intelligence Units, which staged
during November at the Technical Intelligence Depot, moved
forward during December and January to join divisions participating in the M-1 (Luzon) operation:

> Technical Intelligence Unit No. 4, 6th Division
> Technical Intelligence Unit No. 5, 43d Division
> Technical Intelligence Unit No. 6, 37th Division
> Technical Intelligence Unit No. 7, 40th Division

The Technical Intelligence Depot at Finschhafen is Closed: 28 Feb 1945

With the opening of the Luzon operation, steps were taken
to close down the Depot at Finschhafen and to prepare to move
the entire shipping and receiving sections and six analysis
laboratories (except for a rear-echelon force) to Manila, Luzon,
Philippine Islands, when it should be taken.

In the meantime, team personnel remaining at the Depot
were trained under supervision of team commanders with the
assistance of analysis section chiefs, while analysis section
personnel were occupied principally with writing technical
reports and disposing of captured equipment on hand in preparation for the contemplated move. They crated equipment
that would be needed and as additional tools and instruments
were acquired, chests were constructed, labeled and stored.
Only the minimum requirements in tools were retained in the
shops as operating equipment.

Personnel from the various analysis sections made a trip
to Sio, New Guinea, (Map Incl 1) to obtain enemy materiel
which had been left there by the Japanese approximately ten
months before. British Civil Affairs units were of great
assistance in this operation.

Eighteen Eighth Army Technical Intelligence officers and
men moved forward by air during January to join units in the
field. Vehicles and equipment of these teams were safehanded
later when shipping space was available.

The Assistant Coordinator of Technical Intelligence,
USASOS, Capt Birleffi, and the Ordnance Intelligence officer,
same Headquarters, Major Wilkes, visited the Technical Intelligence Depot in January to expedite forward movement of Technical Intelligence teams. They brought with them a shipment
of speed graphic cameras for use in the field and in the sections, to facilitate preparation of technical reports.

Operations at the Technical Intelligence Depot, Finschhafen, ceased 28 February 1945. All analysis and organizational equipment was readied for immediate shipment to the new
depot area in Manila. Loading commenced 6 March and the detachment was scheduled to sail 12 March.

The closing of the Technical Intelligence Depot necessitated turning over approximately thirty-five tons of captured
equipment to the Ordnance Officer, Base "F". Complete arrangements were made for expediting the loading of this equipment
by the first available water transportation.

Captain Octave F. D. Thomas, Office of the Assistant Executive S-2, Base "F", served as Captured Enemy Equipment
Officer for the base and maintained liaison with the Ordnance

C H A P T E R VII

OPERATIONS ON LUZON

January 1945 -- February 1945

Although the Leyte operation was a bold and decisive
stroke, it was only a small part of the whole Philippine campaign. On the 25th October 1944, five days after the landing
on Leyte, the 1st Cavalry Division struck again at Samar.
(Map Incl 16 and 17) On 15 December the next strategic landing was made on Mindoro, 288 miles northwest of Leyte, (Map
Incl 16 and 17) by the 503d Parachute Infantry reinforced.
As the paratroopers landed on Mindoro they encountered little
Jap resistance, although Tokyo radio proclaimed Mindoro the
key to "control of tomorrow's military situation".

On 5 January 1945 Marinduque was taken with little opposition in the interval between Mindoro and Luzon by elements of
Sixth Army in the first move to clear the Sibuyan Sea. (Map
Incl 18) Then on 9 January, 82 days after Leyte, 600 ships
of an armada carrying Sixth Army troops appeared in the Lingayen Gulf, 100 miles to the northwest of Manila (Map Incls
16 and 18) the point of the initial Japanese landing in the
Philippines in December 1941.

With the Seventh Fleet aircraft acting as cover, a 15
mile beachhead was secured and soon expanded to over 40 miles.
In five days, more than 400 square miles had been retaken and
armored columns were on the move toward Manila along the three
highways leading to the south.

Capture of Urdaneta opened the northern section of the
Manila-Baguio Highway 5 and snapped the enemy's supply line
through the central Luzon plain. Tarlac, road and rail center of the central plain was overrun. (Map Incl 18)

Manila lay straight ahead, and it developed into a race
to see who would arrive there first, the 1st Cavalry Division
or the 37th Division. As the 37th moved rapidly down Highway
3 from San Fernando and the 1st Cavalry drove down Highway 5,
the race was on. (Map Incl 18)

On 3 February at midnight the 1st Cavalry Division's advanced units crashed the gates of Santa Tomas internment camp and Bilibid Prison in Manila, releasing 5,000 internees.

The Fall of Manila

The battering down of the gates of Santa Tomas by 1st Cavalry troops heralded the opening of the battle for Manila. No more unorthodox battle was ever fought and seldom had such a fanatic foe been encountered.

A mixed army of from 16,000 to 18,000 men defended the city. The units involved consisted of a strange array of hospital patients, air corps personnel, officer candidates, naval personnel from the sunken shipping in the harbor, newly inducted civilians and the like. These troops were organized into provisional units of company or battalion size. Roughly two-thirds of this heterogenous fighting force consisted of naval personnel and one-third of army troops. Army organizational equipment of the defenders was supplemented by armament from the battered planes from the surrounding airfields, and from the sunken ships in the harbor.

Enemy troops totaled about 18,000. As these forces had been committed to defend Manila to the end, little attempt was made to withdraw into the hills to the east. With minor exceptions they fought to the death according to the original plan of defense.

Nor had any plans been formulated for the evacuation of the civilian population. Rather, they were used by the Japanese as best suited their tactical needs: As screens against attacking troops, for barter, and as a means to enable their forces to infiltrate the American lines.

Manila was taken in thirty-five days. The mission of delaying the United States forces had cost the enemy 17,000 counted dead and had left modern Manila a shambles.

After the Fall of Manila

After the fall of Manila, the remaining Japanese in the area retired to a previously constructed defense system to the east. This was the formidable Shimbu Line. In March, elements of the 1st Cavalry Division and the 6th and 43d Infantry Divisions began a strong thrust which finally cracked the line.

The Japs, however, still remained entrenched around two dams, Ipo and Wawa, which stored a major portion of Manila's water supply. On 17 May Ipo fell. (Map, Incl. 18) The blow was so unexpected that the Japs failed to demolish the dam with their previously planted explosives. Later in May, the 38th closed in on Wawa and also secured that dam intact.

In the meantime, the area south of Manila, to the extreme southern tip of Luzon, was gradually cleared of organized resistance.

Recapitulation of Technical Intelligence Organization with Sixth Army

A proper understanding of Technical Intelligence at this point in the war requires a recapitulation of the manner in which it had evolved in its organization and its relationship to the Armies. The Technical Intelligence Field Unit was the basic organization of Technical Intelligence. The Field Unit was composed of Technical Intelligence Teams selected from each of the six major branches of service concerned with supply. One officer and two enlisted men normally composed a T. I. Team. During the Luzon operation there were generally six teams to a unit. The senior officer from those on the various teams functioned as the officer in charge of the unit.

Initially, in the Luzon operation, a unit was attached to each division and, acting under division G-2, operated only in the division area. Liaison between G-2 and the unit was one of the functions of the officer in charge and each team in turn maintained liaison with its respective branch of service at division headquarters. Operating in this fashion, all enemy materiel captured was processed by trained personnel. Certain items of equipment requiring labatory analysis were collected by the team and shipped to the Technical Intelligence Field Depot Unit. It was the function of the Depot Unit to operate a provisional depot in the field until the United States Army Technical Intelligence Depot was permanently established in the Philippines.

Experience demonstrated that the original assignment of the units to divisions had a tendency to make this type of work inelastic. It became the practice in the middle of this operation, as units were released from the divisions, to assign them to corps, and for them to function under corps G-2 and staff officers. This practice made available the entire corps area to the unit rather than the comparatively small division area. In addition, one unit was assigned as a Sixth Army Headquarters Unit. By making this shift, the efficiency was immeasurably increased.

HISTORY OF TECHNICAL INTELLIGENCE

Based on the experience gained in the early phase of the
Luzon operation, it was decided that the Technical Intelligence
Unit should not necessarily include Quartermaster and Medical teams
as there was not sufficient work to warrant their inclusion in
every unit. One Quartermaster and one Medical officer assigned to
operate directly under the control of the coordinating office
(the corps G-2) was sufficient. Sixth Army Technical Intelligence
units on later operations consisted only of Ordnance, Engineer,
Signal Corps and Chemical Warfare personnel.

Technical Intelligence Unit activities reports were submitted
monthly through G-2 channels. Technical reports were widely disseminated. Copies were forwarded directly to the various Chiefs
of Service, USASOS, with information copies made available to G-2.
Many of the technical reports were published in the Technical Intelligence Section of the Sixth Army G-2 Weekly Report prepared by
the Sixth Army Technical Intelligence Coordinator.
Tests made by the T.I. teams were made available to all concerned
and were of immediate tactical value to the Sixth Army Special
Intelligence Section and to guerrilla units operating with
captured equipment.

Besides writing the usual number of reports for dissemination
to the front line troops through the G-2 weekly reports of the
corps to which they were assigned, personnel of the Technical Intelligence units prepared and administered training programs on the
use and repair of enemy equipment for Sixth Army combat troops.

One ordnance technician was placed on duty with Special
Intelligence, Sixth Army, to collect and repair weapons and other
equipment to be issued to guerrilla forces.

In areas under operational control of the Commanding General,
Sixth Army (distinguished from areas under control of the Commanding General. USASOS, or recognized civil government,) decision for
disposition of salvaged materiel was made by Sixth Army in all but
the following cases:

Technical Intelligence agencies were authorized to withdraw for Intelligence and training purposes any items of
captured supplies and equipment. They were advised promptly
of the location of captured material and were given first
priority for removal of necessary items.

Captured food, clothing, and medical supplies and equipment were passed to control of Philippine Civil Affairs Unit
(PCAU) after the Technical Intelligence officer with the
capturing unit signified termination of his interest in these
items.

70

Commanders of capturing corps, divisions or other major
independent units commanded by general officers, utilized any
captured supplies and equipment considered by them necessary
for the prosecution of immediate combat.

Technical Intelligence on Luzon

Field Units Nos. 1, 2, 3, 4, 5, 6 and 7 took part in the
initial stages of the Luzon operation and later were supplemented
or relieved by new teams. (Personnel comprising these and other
units that operated on Luzon are shown in Incl 3). Capt Creed,
recovered from his shrapnel wound, again took over as Coordinator
of Technical Intelligence and Capt Sternal, who had been Acting
Sixth Army T. I. Coordinator, joined one of the teams in the field.

Due to the rapid advance of United States troops on Luzon,
vast quantities of materiel were captured by the Technical Intelligence field units, including many new items of Japanese equipment.
More information was made available to tactical commanders concerning this newly discovered enemy equipment, particularly Ordnance,
than in any previous operation.

In the course of their regular Technical Intelligence activities, members of the various teams collected data which supplied
information on Japanese manufacturers, locations of Japanese Army
units, and the names of other individuals and organizations that
had donated supplies to the enemy army. Many items were discovered,
such as records, manuals, paybooks, diaries, and maps, which were
turned over to CIC or to ATIS for information and translation.

T. I. Field Unit No. 3: Technical Intelligence Field Depot Unit

Field Unit No. 3 again acted as the provisional depot unit
in Luzon as it had done in the Leyte operation. The advance section
of this Unit left Leyte and arrived at San Fabian (Map, Incl 18)
in the Lingayen Gulf region, Luzon, on 11 January 1945, but was
later moved to San Jacinto, Pangasinan Province, as Sixth Army
troops moved rapidly inland. Here, the provisional depot remained
until it was possible to establish the United States Army Technical Intelligence Depot in Manila.

Besides acting as a depot unit, this unit covered the 25th
Division sector in the early stages of the Luzon operation. Engineer Team No. 3 (Capt Johnson, T/5 Garrett, Pvt Carson) recovered
a quantity of mines, of which some were stored for shipment to the
Depot at Finschhafen and others were released to Sixth Army units
to be used for training purposes. Medical Team No. 1 (Capt Able) of
this unit recovered a variety of drugs from small Medical dumps
scattered throughout the area and turned them over to PCAU to be
used for civilian relief.

In February, Field Unit No. 3 Moved to the provisional depot from San Jacinto to Angeles, Pampanga Province, Luzon, but left the materiel that had been collected at San Jacinto to be forwarded later to the regular Technical Intelligence Depot to be established at Manila. The original plan of maintaining a depot at San Jacinto proved to be unfavorable as equipment received from the teams was being taken further away from Manila instead of working toward that city as originally planned. The depot unit attempted to keep contact with the various units, but distances became too great.

By this time quite a few changes had been made in the personnel of the Depot Unit: Capt Bess had been wounded by rifle fire while attempting to render unusable a Japanese 12" howitzer and had been evacuated to Leyte; all other personnel had returned to the Technical Intelligence Depot except Capt Nowakowski, T/Sgt Peterson, and T/5 Moore, of Ordnance; T/5 Garrett and Pfc Carson, Engineers; and T/5 Mangiaracina, Chemical Warfare, he also returned to the Depot shortly thereafter; later, Lt Abbott was added to this group.

From their new location, Clark Field and the country surrounding Angeles were readily accessible. Much equipment had been buried by the Japanese in this vicinity so that in addition to their usual duties at the depot, Field Unit No. 3 had considerable field work to handle, operating sometimes under enemy fire.

Shortly after the Depot had been established in Manila, Japanese materiel recovered in Luzon during preceeding operations was brought in to the Manila Depot from San Jacinto, where the advance field depot had been temporarily in operation; the field depot unit which had moved to Angeles however, was temporarily maintained to facilitate the handling of the flow of captured enemy materiel coming in at that time.

To supplement their transportation facilities, the Angeles Depot team repaired a personnel carrier by going out and finding another one so that parts could be obtained. The team also broke down two Japanese directors, reporting on the inferior machining parts. All materiel collected, (mopping up operations during March produced only a moderate quantity of captured equipment), was brought up to condition and shipped to the Technical Intelligence Depot at Manila or to the United States.

During April, Lt Abbott returned to the Depot at Manila, and Capt Nowakowski, before being reassigned to Ordnance Team No. 7 Technical Intelligence Unit No. 9, was hospitalized for yellow jaundice. With no officer present, T/Sgt Peterson, ranking NCO, was in charge of the temporary depot until June, when 2d Lt Wendell Webster, Engineer, was sent from the United States Army Technical Intelligence Depot into Headquarters, Sixth Army, to evacuate the equipment remaining at the provisional depot at Angeles. Lt Webster was assisted by T/5 Garrett and Pfc Carson, the rest of the personnel at that time returning to the Technical Intelligence Depot at Manila.

T. I. Field Unit No. 7: 40th Division

Field Unit No. 7 was attached to the 40th Division early in December 1944 at Cape Gloucester, New Britain. The division left New Britain 9 December to conduct a dry-run landing operation at Manus Island in the Admiralties. They landed at Lingayen beach 9 January, D-Day, at 1900 hours, under AA fire, with enemy planes flying low over the LST they were aboard. By 29 January they had advanced as far as Bambau, where stubborn enemy resistance from well-fortified caves slowed down their advance.

This unit, like all others in the field during operations, accompanied combat patrols so they would be on hand when equipment was recovered, and considerable Intelligence materiel for all the services was uncovered in the Ft Stotsenburg and Clark Field areas, although many of the supplies had been looted by the civilians.

T. I. Field Unit No. 6: 37th Division

Personnel of Field Unit No. 6 landed at Lingayen Gulf 22 and 23 January.

After reporting to G-2 of Sixth Army, the Unit joined the 37th Division at Concepcion on 27 January 1945, and operated with this division on the drive down Highway No. 3 all the way from that point through the Manila operation.

No enemy Chemical Warfare equipment was uncovered by CWS Team No. 3 (Lt Max L. Hibbs, T/5 James P. Garner) in the 37th Division sector until the Unit reached Clark Field and Fort Stotsenburg, outside of Manila, and then no more until they entered Manila. One medium sized dump was discovered in the Manila area by this team, but the remaining Japanese Chemical equipment was located in small quantities throughout the city.

Apparently the Japanese were well supplied with smoke bombs and incendiaries. The latter were used with good effect in portions of Manila already taken by United States troops, for there was no enemy air activity in the Manila sector after the entry of United States forces.

During the early days of the battle for Manila, a laxity of gas discipline was noted among the enemy troops, evidenced by the fact that few Japanese casualties were carrying their gas masks. During the latter stages of the Manila operation, however, good gas discipline was apparent. No war gases, other than a limited supply of toxic smoke, were used, and it was believed that the Japanese were not capable of initiating or maintaining chemical warfare. It was further deduced that the enemy did not anticipate the United States Army intiating the use of war gases.

Arrangements were made for Capt Clyde R. Woodworth to operate with the 37th Division Surgeon's office. The Manila area was covered as sections of it fell, except the portion immediately around Intramuros, Intramuros, itself, and the port area. Enemy materiel recovered consisted of approximately 200 items of drugs not listed in the manual, "Japanese Drugs and Medicine", and miscellaneous items consisiting of medical notes and pharmaceutical texts written in Japanese. No large dumps were found, however. According to Filipino accounts, the primary cause was the fact that the enemy did not have extensive supplies of either Medical equipment or drugs. Another important factor was that Medical materiel not burned by the retreating Japanese was looted promptly by the natives.

Ordnance Team No. 3 of this Unit (Capt William E. Winterstein, T/4 Winn) conducted firing tests on a newly recovered and very important type 4, 20 cm and a 44.7 cm rocket launcher. Capt Winterstein's reports on these rockets were later published by Sixth Army and by the War Department.

Signal Team No. 3 (Lt Daniels, T/4 Robert R. Apgar, Jr, T/4 Max A. Bratt) located at the Manila Golf Course a transmitter station, the equivalent of the U. S. Press Wireless Corporation. Another radio station was located in the San Miguel Brewery, where other equipment of Intelligence value was recovered. At the Union Theological Seminary, burned-out Signal equipment, part of the Japanese 5KW short wave radio telegraph receiving equipment, was discovered.

Major General Robert S. Beightler, Commanding General of the
37th Infantry Division, wrote a letter of commendation on the
activities of this unit to the Commanding General, USASOS, (Incl 19),
commending their enthusiasm, energy and initiative while working
under considerable hazards from enemy fire, mines and booby traps.
He wrote that through their efforts much equipment and many supplies
which would have otherwise been lost were obtained. He further
stated that in a number of cases the first information on items
of Japanese Ordnance and other equipment was obtained through the
efforts of the teams comprising Technical Intelligence Unit No. 6,
citing particularly the 447 mm rocket, first encountered in Manila.

T.I. Field Unit No. 1; XI Corps

Field Unit No. 1 reported to 38th Division, Eighth Army, staging
on Leyte for the Luzon operation, and secured permission to go into
the field where they operated in the 7th and 77th Divisions'
sectors.

During the greater part of January 1945 the Unit was preparing for the M-7 operation. On D-Day, 29 January, they landed with
the 38th Division at La Paz, Zambales, Luzon. As there was no opposition, the 38th moved rapidly forward and the Field Unit set up
location on the Costolajos airstrip on the night of 30 January.

The next day all the teams of Unit No. 1 were placed on temporary duty with G-2, XI Corps in conformity with the policy of
shifting T.I. units under corps rather than division headquarters.
XI Corps headquarters was in command of the entire operation and
allowed complete coverage by the teams in their search for new
items of enemy equipment. The corps at that time was directing the
operation of the 38th Division and the 34th Regimental Combat Team
of the 24th Division, whose mission was to cut off Bataan Penninsula
and to join forces with the XIV Corps coming down from the north.

The mission, from the Technical Intelligence standpoint, was
not too successful, as little equipment of Intelligence value was
collected. Therefore the Unit was directed by Eighth Army to return to Leyte to prepare for another operation. They left from
Subic Bay, arriving at Eighth Army Headquarters on 15 February,
with only one day to prepare for another operation. They loaded
the following day to join the task force for the next operation.

75

T. I. Field Unit No. 2: 1st Cavalry Division

Field Unit No. 2 was attached to the 1st Cavalry Division on 8 February 1945, and operated in and around Manila and the hills to the east of that city. The only member of Ordnance Team No. 11, Capt. Sternal, although handicapped by lack of enlisted men did locate several important Ordnance items. These included quantities of practically every type of ammunition. From shell fragments he identified the type of artillery being used against United States troops and by the same method was able to determine that the enemy was using an 8" rocket. Reports were also made of dumps of enemy ammunition which could be made available to United States troops.

Chemical Warfare Team No. 4 (Capt William J. Roberts, Sgt Charles B. Gates, T/5 Paul R. Going), which had flown with vehicles and equipment 23 December to join I Corps, was assigned the mission of conducting a survey on the status of Japanese Chemical Warfare munitions in Manila. Intelligence had reports that several places in that city had been used a storage for these munitions. The investigation, corroborating that of others CWS Intelligence teams in the Manila area, showed that non-lethal Chemical Warfare munitions and protective equipment had been used in moderate quantities in and around Manila but not in large enough quantities to indicate that the Japanese were prepared offensively or defensively for Chemical Warfare.

Throughout the entire Philippine Campaign, Engineer Intelligence teams did a large amount of mine removal work when it expedited combat action, rather than wait for Division Engineer troops to clear the areas. The Engineer Intelligence teams and the Engineer Analysis Section also assisted in setting up exhibits and trained Army Divisions on Jap mines and booby traps.

By the end of February, which ended the first period of the Luzon operation, Technical Intelligence personnel on temporary duty to Sixth Army had operated in the central plain of Luzon, Manila, Corrigidor, Bataan and the hills east and southeast of Manila (Map Incl 13).

HISTORY OF TECHNICAL INTELLIGENCE

Technical Intelligence on Luzon After February 1945

All the previously discussed Field Units-- Units 1, 2, 3, 6, and 7 -- had been relieved from field duty by March and returned to the Technical Intelligence Depot for duty with analysis sections. Field Unit No. 5, however, remained on operations with XIV Corps. Three other units were also in the field after March: Field Unit No. 4, which also had participated in the original Luzon landings, assigned to I Corps; Field Unit No. 8, new in the field, also assigned to I Corps; and Field Unit No. 9, newly assigned to XI Corps.

Special T. I. Teams with Sixth Army

Headquarters Sixth Army, located at San Fernando, Pampanga Province, instituted an extensive training course on enemy equipment for its troops during the month of May. Altogether, nine Technical Intelligence teams, designated as "Enemy Equipment and Materiel Instruction Teams", participated in this program, conducted under the direction of the AC of S, G-3.

The groups included: Chemical Warfare Team No. 2 from Field Unit No. 4; Engineer Team No. 6 from Field Unit No. 8; three Ordnance teams -- 5, 7, and 11 -- composed of personnel from Field Units 5, 8, and 9; and three Signal teams -- 1, 2, and 4 -- from Field Units 9, 4, and 5, respectively.

In addition to Units 4, 5, 8, and 9 that were in the field during April, and the Enemy Equipment and Materiel Instruction teams, there were added two individual teams operating directly under Sixth Army G-2 on special assignments. Instead of being confined to certain sectors, these teams covered all areas occupied by Sixth Army combat units on Luzon.

To assist the guerrilla forces in Northern Luzon in locating, collecting and repairing items of equipment, T/3 Lischalk and Pvt Thevenot, Ordnance technicians, functioned as an Enemy Weapons Team working directly under the Special Intelligence Section, Sixth Army Headquarters. Pvt Thevenot was hospitalized some time later, but Sgt Lischalk, aided by his team training in the field, continued to supply the troops with weapons and ammunition. Due to his work considerably quantities of Japanese Ordnance material were utilized by the guerillas in the Northern Luzon area.

The other special team was a JAPLAT Team consisting of T/Sgt Julius L. Horton and Sgt Allen J. Branigan which worked directly out of Sixth Army Headquarters and was assigned to the collection of JAPLAT, code name for nameplates and rubbings from captured enemy equipment. This team processed a large quantity of name plates daily for transmittal to AS of S, G-2, USASOS, from whom they were sent to the Director of Intelligence, Army Service Forces, Washington (later to The Ground Industry Section, MIS, Washington).

This team, which successfully expedited the collection of nameplates was organised in conformity with USAF's letter, FEGB-386.3, Subject: Nameplates and Serial Number Data from Captured Japanese Materiel other than aircraft, dated 3 February 1945 (Incl 20). This letter delegated responsibility for the collection and processing of name plates and markings on captured enemy equipment in SWPA to the Commanding General, USASOS, and directed Technical Intelligence personnel to collect and advise thecommands to which they were attached on processing nameplates and marking data.

Since the Office of the AS of S, G-2, USASOS, was responsible for the coordination of Technical Intelligence activites, the S-2 offices of various vases in the Philippines were designated the coordinating agencies for Technical Intelligence whihin those bases, officer was appointed at each base with Technical Intelligence including responsibility for collection of JAPLAT, as his sole function (letter, GSBT-386.3, Headquarters USASOS, Subject: Nameplates and Technical Intelligence, dated 13 February 1945 (Incl 21).

T. I. Field Unit No. 5: I & XIV Corps

T. I. Field Unit No. 5 had landed on white Beach No. 3 at the town of San Fabian, with the 43rd Division the morning of D-Day. During the period of 9 to 31 January this Unit operated in the 43rd and occasionally in the 25th Divisions' areas, both in Cavite Province, south of Manila.

On 1 February the Unit was placed on temporary duty with I Corps, continuing with the 43rd and some teams with the 32nd and 33rd Divisions. On 24 February they were relieved from duty with Sixth Army to be sent to XIV Corps, operating in Batangas Province in Southern Luzon east of Lake Taal, where contacts were made with the 1st Cavalry and the 11th Airborne Divisions.

Chemical Warfare Team No. 7 (Capt Lary, Sgt Branigan, T/4 Mooney) of Field Unit No.5, collected a considerable quantity of Jap equipment in the 43d and later in the 33d and 32d Divisions' sectors. This included: protective clothing, flame throwers, maintenance and testing kits, detector dits, smoke candles and gas masks of various types.

There seemed to be no systematic laying of mine fields in the 43d Division sector. A few tape measure mines were found lying on the concrete highway, but they were poorly concealed and easly recognized. Others, not so easily detected, were placed in broken spots in the pavement. At night, infiltration parties planted mines and depth charges at bridges and along the shoulders of previously cleared roads, which resulted in some casualties and made it necessary to resweep the roads every morning.

Several booby traps reported by civilians to PCAU were removed or neutralized by the Engineer Intelligence Team (Capt Jordan A. Hamner T/4 Roger W. Sherwood, and Pvt Emile M. Turcotte). Later, because of the enemy's use of mines and booby traps, a report on their description and method of neutralization was submitted by the team to 43d Division G-2 and thence to the S-2 of all battalions and regiments.

In the 11th Airborne area a great deal of heavy Engineering equipment of all types was recovered, including diesel and gasoline engines, air compressors, searchlights, concrete mixers, well drilling rigs, steel sharpeners, lathes, bull dozers, road rollers, gasoline locomotives and many other items. Also, thousands of mines, mostly bombs, shells and depth-charges with pressure igniters, were found in this area. Many yardstick, flower pot, conical boat, and lunge mines with a light metal shell, were also found throughout this area.

Medical Team No. 5 (Capt Frederick B. Thompson, Lt James L. Molthan) recovered the following items, which were either put to use for United states troops or turned over to PCAU for civilian use: a portable X-Ray unit, 2 portable surgical tables, a culture incubator, and numerous drugs and dressings.

Ordnance Intelligence Team No.5 (Lt Philip A. Wurzel, Pvt Ben T. Garcia) in December was attached temporarily to 43rd Division, but on completion of landing operations on D-Day, worked independently as a team located at San Jacinto, Luzon. San Jacinto made a convenient base for short trips into the surrounding operational areas, where considerable equipment was recovered. By request of G-2 33d Division, this team submitted an instructive report on Japanese tactics and equipment used in the Luzon area which was disseminated to the troops. This team also turned over assorted items of Intelligence value to the Depot and released a few weapons to the Coordinator of Technical Intelligence for guerrilla supply.

In April, they were joined by Capt Sternal. Previous to this Capt Sternal had operated alone as the only team in the field from Field Unit No.2. He had been in contact with the enemy east of Manila throughout March, except for a ten-day rest period. He resumed operations on the 25th of March and then was transferred in April to Field Unit No. 5 as officer in charge of the Unit.

In May, this personnel was transferred to Headquarters Sixth Army, again operating as Ordnance Team No. 5 with T/5 Sterckx (from Field Unit No. 8) added as a second enlisted man; Capt Sternal again headed up Ordnance Team No. 11, assisted by T/4 Blaney and T/5 Gabage from Field Units No.8 and 9 respectively.

Quartermaster Team No.5, (Lt Philip C. Anderson, Pvt Kenneth S, Echerd) uncovered several large food dumps containing the usual rice, fish, crackers and common condiments, which were turned over to the 43d Division Quartermaster and PCAU for distribution to the civilian population.

Signal Team No. 4 (Lt William F. Howind, T/3 Kurt H. Richter, T/4 Julius J. Matto) covered the 43d Division region south of Manila during January and February, securing, along with other equipment, a suitcase radio evidently intended for espionage work. This item was reported through the XIV Corps G-2 Periodic Report. In June, this team was transferred to Headquarters Sixth Army as one of the Enemy Equipment and Material Instuction Teams.

The Chemical Warfare, Engineer and Medical teams from this Unit returned to the Depot early in March. The rest of the teams, with the exception of those transferred to Headquarters Sixth Army, returned on 25 April.

T. I. Field Unit No. 4: I Corps

While Manila was being captured to the south, United States Forces wheeled and struck northward toward Baguio, around which centered one of the most bitterly protracted battles of the entire campaign. The city fell on 29 April. Ahead lay Balete Pass, controlling the approaches to the Cagayan Valley, Japanese bread basket in the Philippines.

Field Unit No. 4 which had landed in the Lingayen Gulf area on D-Day, was attached to I Corps, working in the 6th, 25th, 33d, and 37th Divisions' sectors. Considerable equipment and materiel were recovered as the Unit worked its way up the Lingayen Valley. During February, this Unit also aided in conducting a short course on Japanese equipment for armored units under I Corps.

Chemical Warfare Team No. 2 (Capt Paul J. Walsh, T/4 Robert J. Showman, T/5 Raymond D. Gaddo) of this unit supplied information to Headquarters, I Corps, which enabled them to make an estimate of the enemy Chemical Warfare situation, including: the percentage of enemy troops carrying gas masks and protective clothing; a notation of the presence of Chemical Warfare munitions and devices used in offensive action; a record of the gas-proofing of enemy emplacements; and a report on the fact that Japanese tanks and holding detachments were carrying smoke candles for screening purposes. With the exception of common type smoke candles, however, this team found little Chemical Warfare equipment. In May, T/4 Showman was recalled to the Technical Intelligence Depot, and Capt Walsh and Sgt Gaddo were transferred to Headquarters, Sixth Army, to instruct in Chemical Warfare with the Enemy Equipment and Materiel Instruction Teams conducting the Sixth Army training program.

Engineer Team No. 1 (Major Harwood, T/3 Ellyett, T/3 Paris), in addition to their routine recovery of enemy equipment, discovered and neutralized the new type sack mine and many improvised mines and booby traps. The reports edited by this team for dissemination to front line units on precautions and instructions in handling improvised Jap booby traps were instrumental in preventing casualties in the divisions in which they were serving. If communications had been better, lives would also have been saved in the 24th Division, which had at least two casualties from sack mines and suffered concurrent damage to equipment.

Several items of enemy Ordnance, of which little was known, were discovered in the 6th Infantry Division's sector by Ordnance Team No. 1 (Capt Pope, Pfc Wm J. Peters, Pvt Robert M. DeFrietas). These included flame throwing guns and tanks, and a type 90, 75 mm high velocity field gun. Other improvements and new type Ordnance noted: an increased number of medium artillery guns (105 mm and 150 mm caliber) over the lighter calibers (70 mm and 75 mm types); also increased amounts of 105 and 150 mm ammunition.

Enemy stores of food which were taken were turned over to the Philippine Civil Affairs Units, who in turn distributed them to needy natives. No large food dumps or dumps of new equipment were encountered by Quartermaster Team No. 1 (Lt Roy H. Curry and Pvt Harold E. Abbott) and small dumps were rapidly looted by the Filipinos. Around Baguio, in the 33d and 37th Division sectors, the team recovered a few Quartermaster items of common type, the quantity and style of items recovered plainly indicating the lack of supplies of the enemy: items such as raincoats and blankets showed evidence of wear and were evidently reclaimed, washed, patched, and reissued by the Japs; American-made GI shoes that had been captured had the uppers cut away and the edges remade so that they also might be re-issued to the Japanese.

Signal Team No. 2 (Capt Fred D. Kierstead, T/Sgt Robert J. McConkie, T/5 Estill C. Micklesimer) found little Signal equipment until the fall of Baguio. Here, large quantities of equipment were recovered from caves and other storage points. Some radios were turned over to United States troops, and one, a model 94 Mark 6 radio set, was used by the 37th Division for intercept work. A Japanese public address system with a 100-watt output, complete with a dynamic speaker, was installed in a command and reconnaissance car by personnel of this team for use by the Sixth Army Psychological Warfare Branch. The bulk of the captured equipment was shipped to the Technical Intelligence Depot. In June, this entire team was transferred to Headquarters Sixth Army, as one of the Enemy Equipment and Materiel Instruction Teams.

HISTORY OF TECHNICAL INTELLIGENCE

T.I.Field Unit No. 8: I Corps

Of the seven original Field Units that had launched the operations in Southern Luzon, only Field Units 4 and 5 remained in the field during March and April. The rest were returned to the United States Army Technical Intelligence Depot and were replaced by Field Units 8 and 9.

Field Unit No. 8 left Finschhafen on 5 March 1945, just before the Depot closed in preparation for the transfer to Manila. As the Unit was new in the field, it operated in conjunction with Field Unit No.4 until the end of March, and as in the case of new personnel, a good deal of its time was absorbed at first in becoming familiar with field operations in preparation for future assignments.

Field Unit No. 8, acting upon instructions of G-2, I corps, operated with the 32d and 25th Divisions in the Villa Verde Trail and Balete Pass areas of Northern Luzon from 24 March on through April. In addition to their regular duties, all sections of this Unit cooperated to collect numerous items of enemy equipment to be added to the I Corps Information and Education Center's display.

CWS Team No. 13 (1st Lt Louis Mocny, M/Sgt Benjamin A Becker, T/5 Charles H. Johnson) of this Unit had spent considerable time contacting the Chemical Warfare officers of I Corps, including division officers, in order to concur with a new procedure of operation for CWS Technical Intelligence teams as directed by the Chemical officers of sixth Army and I Corps.

In March, M.Sgt Becker received a head wound as a result of the accidental discharge of a 45 caliber pistol, and was evacuated from the area.

Engineer Team No.6 (Lt Frank J.DiPhillips, Pvt Rudy G.Colby, Pvt Eugene F. Weins) found a considerable quantity of mines and booby traps. They were called upon to familiarize the troops with this equipment and to submit reports which were published by G-2 for the interest of all concerned. Later in May they were called in to Sixth Army Headquarters to assist in the Enemy Equipment and Materiel Instruction Teams' training program.

The medical officer, Lt John B.Muddiman, operated in conjunction with Field Units 4 and 5, in the I Corps sector. Samples of 195 Japanese medicinals and laboratory reagents were recovered, together with samples of Japanese medical, surgical, dental, and X-Ray equipment recovered from around Baguio. Lt Muddiman also identified the enemy drugs stored at PCAU hospitals within the I Corps sector to permit their use by PCAU physicians.

Ordnance Team No.9 (Lt Glenn E. Oman,Sgt Warren D. Blaney, T/5 Allen M.Storckx) recovered a considerable amount of enemy Ordnance,including several aircraft machine guns which had been used in ground combat. Some of this equipment was turned in to Ordnance companies for repair and the remainder was turned over to a collecting company. Many of these repaired Japanese machine guns were turned on the enemy by United States and Philippine Army units in later battles.

Lt Oman returned to the Technical Intelligence Depot in May. T/5 Storckx reported to Sixth Army to work with Lt Wurzel and Pfc Garcia on Ordnance Team No. 5 and T/4 Blaney reported to Capt Sternal on Ordnance Team No.11. Both teams participated in the Sixth Army Enemy Equipment and Materiel Instruction program.

The quartermaster section had little luck recovering equipment as no enemy dumps of quartermaster significance were captured along the Villa Verde Trail or in the Balete Pass areas,though miscellaneous items were recovered.Due to the limited activity concerning enemy Quartermaster items.Capt Robert S.Gunderson,Pvt Ponciano Loredo,Pvt Michael J. Piccoli,of this team devoted much of their time to assisting the Ordnance team. However,some research on United States Quartermaster items was completed.

T.I. Field Unit No.9 XI Corps

Field unit No.9 was attached to XI Corps operating in the central Luzon sector. All six services comprised the teams of this Unit.

CWS Intelligence Team No.14 (Capt Russel T.Werby,Cpl William H.Davidson,Pfc George B.Reagan),covering the 28th and 43d Division areas,found some new equipment.

Good examples of Japanese heavy Engineer equipment were located by Engineer Team No.6 (Lt Frank G. Pospisil,S/Sgt Richard T.Smith, Pvt Frank M. Ledesma).

The Medical officer,Lt Earl D.Raab,recovered some Medical materiel from a large supply dump: a microscope,an anesthesian machine,alcohol,miscellaneous bandages and dressings,lysol,a dental kit,a water purifier,and assorted quantities of drugs and medicines. Non-expendable items were processed through the technical Intelligence Depot.

Several types of heavy equipment were recovered by Ordnance Team No.8 (Capt Jack K.Palmer,Cpl John P.Smallwood,Pfc Charles R. Kabele) and ordnance Team No.7 (Lt Henry L. Abbott,T/5 Victor J. Gabage,Pfc Robert P.Shinn).This included a 15 cm self-propelled mount,a 70 mm battalion howitzer,a 75 mm gun,a truck and all types of ammunition.Two type 97 Jap tanks mounting 47 mm guns were found.

During March and April, several changes in personnel were made within this team. Pfc Shinn, after a short hospitalization period, was returned to the Technical Intelligence Depot; Capt Palmer was hospitalized for amoebic dysentery; Cpl Gabage was hospitalized for an infected hand; and the two Ordnance teams were combined as Ordnance Team No 7 with Lt. Abbott in charge.

In May, Cpl Sedlwood returned to the Technical Intelligence Depot but Lt Abbott and Pfc Kabele reported to Sixth Army Headquarters as one of the Ordnance teams participating in the Enemy Equipment and Materiel Instruction training program. Cpl Gabage, upon being released from the hospital, also reported to Sixth Army to assist with the training program as part of Capt Sternal's Ordnance Team No. 11.

Many types of Quartermaster equipment were recovered by S/Sgt William J. Foss, Pvt Edward G. Stone and Pvt William Watkins of Quartermaster Team No. 6. As most of these had no Intelligence value, they were turned over to local salvage units for disposition. During April, Pvt Watkins was relieved of duty with this team.

Signal Team No. 1 (T/3 Lotz, Pfc Anderson) found that areas recently evacuated by the enemy yielded only small amounts of Signal equipment. Therefore, in June, Pfc Anderson returned to the Technical Intelligence Depot, Manila, and T/3 Lotz was sent to Sixth Army Headquarters as Signal Team No. 1 in the Enemy Equipment and Materiel Instruction program.

Close of Operations on Luzon

Sixth Army operations in central and northern Luzon during May moved slowly but steadily forward. East of Manila, where the enemy was strongly entrenched, their resistance was stubborn. Ipo and Wawa Dams, which controlled the Manila water supply, were secured intact, however, and the Japanese forces here, as well as in Southern Luzon, were encircled and reduced to remnants by June.

In the north, Baguio fell, and though the Japs staged strong counter-attacks against United States forces along the Villa Verde Trail, they were pushed back from their cave positions along Balete Ridge, and Balete Pass itself was taken.

At the beginning of June, the Cagayan Valley was the only large area in Luzon remaining in enemy hands. A combined American and Philippine force closed in on Aparri, at the northern end of the Cagayan Valley and secured the town without opposition on 21 June. Meanwhile, Sixth Army forces had made pincer drives from Balete Pass at the southern end of the Valley northwest along Highway No. 4 and northeast along Highway No. 5. On 26 June, near Alcala, Sixth Army's 37th Division made contact with leading elements of

the 511th Parachute Infantry which had advanced south along
Highway No. 5 following an airborne invasion near Aparri. This
junction effectively secured the entire length of the Cagayan
Valley. From then to the close of the Luzon operation, which
was terminated by the end of the war, fighting consisted mainly
 in liquidating pockets of enemy resistance which had been by-
passed.

CHAPTER VIII

SOUTHERN PHILIPPINE CAMPAIGN

December 1944 -- August 1945

As the Sixth Army had been assigned the Luzon operation and their full efforts were needed to be focused to the north, the task of cleaning out the Japanese resistance in the Southern Philippines was delegated to Eighth Army (26 December 1944). Though some of the islands had been initially invaded by Sixth Army --Samar, Mindoro, Marinduque -- all of these had to be cleared of Japs (Maps, Incls 16 and 17). In Leyte, Eighth Army had a fine base for future operation.

The Southern Philippine Campaign sonsisted of landing operation after landing operation, some against little opposition, some against fanatical stands by the enemy. One characteristic stood out: each island consisted of a series of pillboxes and cave strong points; each consisted of the same grim and gruelling digging or burning out of the enemy with troops fighting forward by inches against the mud and terrain on many occasions. The fighting developed into a routine of destruction and the cry became to kill until the will of the enemy to resist had been utterly broken. During the following months, Japanese were pushed back in all sections and the Japanese supply lines were cut, forcing the enemy to live off the land. However, the Japanese though gradually liquidated, remained a well organized and well integrated force in the larger areas, maintaining a coordinated and orderly retirement back into the mountains.

Recapitulation of Technical Intelligence Organization with Eighth Army

The administration of Technical Intelligence with Eighth Army was somewhat different than with Sixth Army, Circular 136, Headquarters, Eighth Army, dated 10 May 1945, directed that Technical Intelligence teams attached to that Headquarters would be placed directly under the administrative, operational and technical control of the chiefs of their respective services. When attached to units in the field, the teams worked under and were controlled by the service chiefs of the units to which attached. Close coordination was maintained with G-2 of the Army.

The Eighth Army Technical Intelligence Coordinator, Lt Col Julian, coordinated Technical Intelligence activites with the chiefs of services and acted as an advisor in Technical Intelligence matters.

Correspondence between Eighth Army and G-2, USASOS, and the Commanding Officer, 5250th Technical Intelligence Company, was routed by G-2 channels through the Technical Intelligence Coordinators, Eighth Army.

In addition to the regular field technical reports and monthly activites reports, this circular also provided for the submission of ten-day activites reports by each team. Technical reports approved by chiefs of services were published in the Eighth Army Technical Intelligence Bulletin.

Since Eighth Army operations were smaller in scope than those of the Sixth Army, they necessitated fewer Technical Intelligence personnel. With Sixth Army, the tendency had been, as the operation progressed in Luzon, to relieve the Technical Intelligence units from temporary duty with the divisions and to attach them to corps. In the Southern Philippines this was done to a less extent, for frequently it was necessary to commit only a single division or even a regimental combat team to each operation. When necessary, the number of unit personnel was cut by eliminating certain services but this was held to a minimum so as not to impair the efficiency of the unit.

Although no training program was carried on by the Technical Intelligence teams with Eighth Army, considerable information was passed on to the troops in the form of reports on new equipment recovered. Information concerning enemy use of mines, and descriptions of improvied mines and other Ordnance of immediate combat importance, were disseminated. Equipment for training purposes was also made available to Division units.

Victor 3 -- Palawan: 41st Division

The Technical Intelligence units, instead of being
designated by numbers, were identified according to the
operation in which they participated throughout the Southern
Philippines campaign. Since the assignment of personnel on
temporary duty to the Armies was a prerogative of the Armies
themselves, and since Eighth Army had a definite policy of
mobility for Technical Intelligence personnel, there was
considerable reshuffling of teams under Eighth Army control.
The reorganized Technical Intellignece Unit No. 1 was again
redistributed by Eighth Army and its personnel assigned to
the various Victor operations.

A Technical Intelligence Unit composed of one officer
and two enlisted men was placed on temporary duty with the
41st Division for the V-3 operation against Palawan,
Philippine Islands (Maps, Incls 16 and 17). Personnel of
the Unit were: Capt. Robert J. Ingrahm, T/3 Carl R.
Simmons and Pfc. Walter E. Hawkins. (Complete roster of the
Southern Philippines campaign is included in Incl 3).

On the morning of 28 February 1945, the Unit landed on
Palawan with the 186th Regimental Combat Team of the 41st
Division. Serviceable, standard items of captured
equipment recovered, including generator sets, lathes and
radio repair parts, were turned over to the tactical units
for immediate use. The balance of the equipment was shipped
to Headquarters Eighth Army for inventory and shipment to
the United States Army Technical Intelligence Depot.
Information on the types of booby traps found was given to
the Task Force Intelligence officer.

Victor 4 — Zamboanga, Mindanao: 41st Division

As the Technical Intelligence Unit for Palawan was staging for that operation, a considerably larger Unit was also staging on Mindoro Island with the 41st Division for the V 4 operation against Zamboanga Peninsula, Mindanao, Philippine Islands (Map, Incl 17), personnel of this Unit were:

OCC Intelligence Team

2nd Lt Charles F. Melchor   T/5 Thomas H. Ivory
T/5 William H. Moore

Engineer Intelligence Team

Pvt James W. Stephens

Medical Intelligence Team

1st Lt Travis L. Bowden

Ordnance Intelligence Team

Capt Ernest V. Cameron

Signal Intelligence Team

1st Lt George P. Ford

A week was spent in preparation for embarkation, and on 6 March the group boarded an LST and departed. After an uneventful trip, they arrived on the scene of the empending action on the morning of 10 March. The bombardment that followed was terrific. Finally, at H plus 4, the Unit landed on Red Beach under enemy shell and mortar fire which continued throughout the day.

The Technical Intelligence Unit set up its headquarters on Zamboanga and proceeded to cover all the areas taken by the combat troops. The operation was one in which the supporting units of artillery, mortar and dive bombers played the more important part, with the infantry occupying areas after they have been thoroughly shelled and bombed. The Japs exploited every possible means to supply their troops with weapons and improvised every conceivable item that could be made locally.

This operation yielded a considerable quantity of old and many new weapons never seen before. More and more automotive equipment was captured as the enemy was driven into the interior where the roads were impassable. This equipment, when captured in serviceable condition, was turned over to PCAU to aid in supplying and process- the civilians.

Ground mines were extensively employed in this area and were made from every available material. Included were wooden box mines, type 93 mines, artillery shells rigged as mines, Navy depth charges, torpedo war heads and a new marine mine. As a great deal of this was Navy equipment, the Naval Mobile Explosives Investigation Unit No. 1 was called in to identify and examine it.

Lt Ford found that the Japanese type 97 portable wireless telephone set could receive signals clearly from U. S. frequency modulated SCR-610 and SCR-300 sets at distances of 2000 to 3000 yards. This was important, as messages in the past had frequently been sent in the clear on these two sets. The 41st Division Signal officer, the G-2, and the Division artillery were given this information.

Lt Bowden made trips to all installations held by U. S. troops but very little Medical equipment of technical interest was found. A Filipino doctor stated that the Japanese had taken everything of medical value into the hills.

On the morning of 13 March, as Lt Bowden was proceeding to a guerrilla aid station with two guerrillas and a driver in a weapons carrier, a Japanese machine gun opened fire from the side of the road. Lt Bowden and the driver were both hit. The party proceeded on foot back to Headquarters where the injured were admitted to the 133rd General Hospital.

By the end of March only mopping up operations remained on Zamboanga, and on 31 March the Unit embarked with the Sulu-White force for an operation on Sanga and Bongka Islands of the Sulu Archipelago, (Map Incl 17) Philippine Islands. With this landing, certain members of the Unit had made three D-Day amphibious landings in a little over one month.

No great stocks of equipment were found on this operation and very few new items of equipment. It was noted, though, that some of the equipment taken was of German manufacture and some of it had been made in the United States.

As no new items of equipment were being employed by the enemy, the Technical Intelligence Unit returned to the 41st Division Headquarters, Zamboanga, on 26 April.

During May, Lt Melchor and T/5's Ivory and Moore secured no new Chemical Warfare items in this area, but did recover some interesting older types of equipment

At the end of May, Technical Intelligence personnel who participated on this operation, returned to the Technical Intelligence Depot with the exception of two officers. Capt. Cameron spent the early part of June in the office of the Ordnance Officer, Eighth Army Headquarters, assisting in the establishment of a future operational procedure for Eighth Army Ordnance Technical Intelligence Teams. Upon termination of this temporary duty he returned to X Corps Headquarters to supervise Corps Technical Intelligence teams and to take over as Corps Ordnance Technical Intelligence officer and as officer in charge of Ordnance Team No. 6.

In early July, Capt. Ford reported in to Headquarters Eighth Army for staff work with the Chief Signal Officer. This included, along with other work, preparing a chart showing Japanese electrical Signal instruments with the American counterparts.

Victor 1 -- Panay -- Negros: 40th Infantry Division

The Technical Intelligence Unit attached to the 40th Infantry Division for the Panay operation (Maps, Incl 16 and 17) landed with the combat troops of the Division on D-Day, 18 March, at H plus thirty minutes. Personnel of this Unit were:

CWS Intelligence team

Sgt Harvey Bylsma   Pvt Homer Blankenship

Engineer Intelligence Team

1st Lt William Purnell

Ordnance Intelligence Team

Pvt Nick P. Vannucci

Quartermaster Intelligence Team

Capt Kenneth H. Bowman

Signal Intelligence Team

S/Sgt John P. Kost

HISTORY OF TECHNICAL INTELLIGENCE

Operations were carried on in the vicinity of Iloilo City. Little enemy equipment of Intelligence value was recovered in this operation, and only a few dumps with conventional items of Japanese equipment were uncovered. The Japs, as they evacuated the city of Iloilo, took equipment that was of value with them and burned the rest. The large warehouses along the docks were bare, with the exception of fertilizer and empty beer bottles.

Numerous radios, which were of American commercial make and which had been destroyed beyond repair, were found in the Japanese radio station. A Jap microphone and one radio, a few phonograph records and an electrodynamic speaker were recovered from this station.

S/Sgt Kost, the only man assigned to Signal Intelligence with the 40th Division, received help during May from Signal Team No. 7, regularly with the 24th Division, but little additional Signal equipment was recovered as most of the equipment left behind by the retreating enemy had either been destroyed by them or by U. S. heavy mortar and artillery barrages.

In the town of Tigbauan, Capt Bowman (QM) found a small supply room in a ruined chapel. A few pieces of enlisted men's clothing were collected, together with mixed ammunition and printed matter. There had been a small garrison of Japanese there, and only a limited amount of supplies, other than foodstuffs, was left.

The 40th Division, having secured Panay, shifted its attention to ending the Japanese occupation of Negros, Philippine Islands. The Technical Intelligence Unit with the vision also followed through on this operation, which opened 29 March. On Negros, as on Panay, the enemy made little use of heavy Engineer equipment, and small Engineer items of Japanese make were virtually non-existent. The largest enemy dump secured up to the end of April contained only one Engineer item of technical value, a company size water filtering plant. Lt Purnell was Engineer officer on this operation, with the rest of his team assigned to the 24th Division.

Much of this equipment, both Allied and enemy, recovered on this operation was turned over to the combat troops. Included were American-made gasoline motors, electric generators, lathes, planers, shapers, tools, auto parts, auto tires, gasoline driven road rollers and tractors.

Sgt Bylsma and Pvt Blankenship found practically all Chemical Warfare material encountered on Negros destroyed or damaged. As correctly reported by this, as well as other teams, in the Philippines the Japanese were apparently unprepared to successfully conduct or defend themselves against chemical warfare.

92

Although most of the individual Japanese observed carried gas masks (probably due to the effective use of white phosphorus by United States troops), their shelters were not gas proofed.

In the Dumaguete section of Negros, Oriental, Capt Bowman located some new Quartermaster items, along with the usual quantities of Class B helmets, uniforms, shelter halves, packs, rain coats and rations. New items of special interest were a gasoline tank truck with auxiliary hand pump, an airplane drop container, and an emergency ration composed of soy bean powder compressed into cakes and packaged in waterproof containers.

There were no large concentrations of supplies and equipment on the island, and even in the caves used as emergency supply points, supplies were scant and in disorder. As no attempt at organized supply was apparent, the enemy was evidently living off the land, confiscating food and supplies from the natives.

By the end of June all Technical Intelligence activities for the V-1 operation had been concluded, and all personnel, except Pvt Vannucci, who was transferred to Headquarters X Corps for assignment to Ordnance Team No, 6, had returned to the Technical Intelligence Depot.

Victor 2 -- Cebu: Americal Infantry Division

A Technical Intelligence Unit was attached to the Americal Division on 19 March. Personnel in the new Unit were:

CWS Intelligence Team

Capt Robert Ingrahm

Engineer Intelligence Team

1st Lt John F. Keane   Pvt Christopher W. Tamer

Ordnance Intelligence Team

1st Lt Grady J. Bell, Jr.

Quartermaster Intelligence Team

T/Sgt Eugene F. Rossi

Signal Intelligence Team

T/3 Donald W. Borchers

HISTORY OF TECHNICAL INTELLIGENCE

Embarking with the Division, the Unit reached Cebu, Philippine Islands, (Maps, Incl 16 and 17) on D-Day, 26 March. The landing was made at Talisay, from where the troops moved in to capture Cebu City. Here, Division Headquarters was established.

Capt Ingraham, CWS, investigated the Japanese munition used against United States troops which was reported to give off a greenish, nauseating smoke. Information on the gas had been given to the Division G-2. The investigation indicated that no toxic gasses were being used and the findings were disseminated to the troops to allay any fears concerning the possibility of the enemy's use of such agents.

No large supplies of Chemical Warfare material were found. Items recovered included improvised Molotov cocktails, presumably for use against U. S. tanks, and eight suits of light-weight ruberized protective clothing.

As several improvised weapons and types of explosives were encountered, Lt Bell of Ordnance, made a report to the Division G-2 regarding improvised bombs and demolition charges that were being used in destroying guns. Some of these were found on Japanese who were attempting to infiltrate to American artillery positions. A report was also made on an improvised 130mm mortar. The mortar was apparently a field expedient devised to use the ammunition left behind when large quantities of weapons were taken from Cebu to reinforce Leyte.

Though no new Ordnance equipment was recovered, fourteen very high frequency directional radio transmitters having the same frequency bands as the Unites States VT fuzes were captured near Cebu City. These sets were inspected by T/3 Borchers (Signal) and arrangements made in conjunction with the Ordnance and Signal officers of Eighth Army Headquarters to have the radios tested in the field with actual AA firing to see if VT fuzes could be activated by waves from these sets, since this would prove an effective counter-measure against Unite States weapons.

Towards the end of May, Lt Bell was transferred to Headquarters X Corps to coordinate Ordnance Technical Intelligence activities in the Mindanao area.

Lt Keane and Pvt Tamer, Engineer Team No. 7, also reported on the number and variety of enemy improvised mines. In addition, two landing field lights with generators mounted on trucks, recovered intact were shipped to the Technical Intelligence Depot minus the generators and trucks which were put to use by Division Ordnance.

The tactical situation by the end of May had reached the point where the enemy had retreated north to the hills, leaving the bulk of their equipment in caves along the road. This equipment was also secured.

During the latter part of the month the team also made an extensive reconnaissance of the facilities in captured areas on Cebu and submitted reports, including one on a cement plant which was found inoperative because of lack of certain mechanical parts for the power plant. The team then travelled to Negros, located necessary parts at a sugar plant, and was negotiating for a loan of these parts when they were recalled to Eighth Army Headquarters. The project was therefore turned over to and completed by Capt Ingrahm.

Neither T/Sgt Rossi, Quartermaster, nor T/3 Borchers, Signal, found large stores of material and equipment. No new items were recovered and most standard items, which were of no technical value, were turned over to the division for its use -- in particular to the Signal Depot to be used as parts in constructing the division broadcasting station, NVAD. Nameplates, as in all cases where equipment was turned over to the troops, were forwarded to the United States Army Technical Intelligence Depot.

The enemy, withdrawing steadily, destroyed all supplies left behind, and it was noted by the end of May that their stocks of materiel were becoming critical, consisting by then mainly of small arms ammunition, and foodstuffs, principally rice and sugar.

By the end of June all personnel present on this operation were returned to the Technical Intelligence Depot with the exception of three men: Lt Keane, transferred to assist Lt Col Julian at Eighth Army Headquarters; T/3 Borchers, who was retained to clear up the unfinished work for the Unit, and who was then assigned to staff work with the Chief Signal Officer at Eighth Army: and Lt Bell, who was transferred to X Corps Headquarters to take charge of a combined Ordnance Team No. 6 which operated in the Serangani Bay area of Mindanao during July with the 24th Division.

Victor 5 -- Mindanao; X Corps, 31st and 24th Divisions

The following Technical Intelligence personnel were assigned to X Corps for the Victor 5 operation:

CWS Intelligence Team

Capt William J. Roberts   Sgt Paul R. Going

Engineer Intelligence Team No. 8 (part)

T/Sgt John G. Barkowski   Pfc Edward Burnstein
Pvt Philip Zarahn

Ordnance Intelligence Team No. 6 (part)

T/3 Carl R. Simmons   Pfc Joseph F. Pollack
Pfc Norton H. Rosen

Quartermaster Intelligence Team

Pvt Jean O. Gonzales   Pvt Bertram L. Leslie
Pvt Theodore D. Lillis

Signal Intelligence Team No. 7

Lt Col Erle H. Julian   1st Lt Alcide Santilli
T/5 Bruce A. Harding   Pfc Walter E. Hawkins

These three officers and twelve enlisted men, representing all services except the Medical Corps, landed at Parang, Mindanao, second largest island in the Philippines (Maps, Incl 16 and 17), on 18 April 1945 and from there proceeded to the X Corps area, where they reported to the G-2. As reconnaissance of the area resulted in the recovery of little material of Intelligence value in the 31st Division area, only four men functioned with that Division, while the remaining eleven operated with the 24th Division around Davao. Prior to the outbreak of the war this area had been the center of Japanese colonization in the Philippines and the largest number of Japanese in the Islands still lived there.

A large Japanese storage dump was located. The materiel, which was distributed among five huts apparently used as living quarters, consisted of rice, ammunition and Signal Equipment, the last being buried in shallow caves. Quantities of food and clothing were found by Pvts Gonzales, Lillis and Leslie and were turned over to PCAU and Quartermaster Salvage.

HISTORY OF TECHNICAL INTELLIGENCE

Turned over to the Surgeon, X Corps, in this same operation,
were four to five tons of captured medical supplies for distribution
to various hospital units for use for civilians and prisoners of
war. Of much practical use were two complete water purification
units mounted on 1½ ton trucks. This captured equipment was used
by troops in X Corps and was shipped to the Technical Intelligence
Depot after it was no longer needed.

T/Sgt Barkowski and Pvts Burnstein and Zarahn (Lt Purnell,
officer in charge of this team was on duty with the 40th Division)
recovered several new Engineer items, some interesting improvised
equipment, and a considerable quantity of standard materiel. Some
of this equipment was put into immediate operations, while all
mines and explosives were collected and later destroyed by Ordnance
authorities since they constituted a hazard to surrounding personnel
and materiel. As the Division moved forward in Southeastern
Mindanao during June, fewer land mines and similar devices were
encountered. Likewise, enemy fortifications and defense systems
showed a tendency toward hasty construction. It was apparent the
enemy did not anticipate a retreat of such depth; however, they
showed appreciation of terrain and utilized it to the best advantage.

T/3 Simmons and Pfcs Pollack and Rosen, operating in the Davao
area, found quantities of Ordnance equipment. As in all other
sectors, the Japs showed a marked ability at improvising weapons
from other cannibalized equipment. Mortars capable of firing
standard 75mm and 4.7" artillery projectiles were made from lengths
of gas pipe. In one sector, twenty of these projectiles were
fired at United States troops and could be seen tumbling through
the air as they approached -- though none exploded.

The Japs also improvised land mines armed with bomb fuzes,
hand grenades made from hollow wooden blocks wrapped with wire,
and others made from gas pipe. They used United States ration
cans filled with picric acid, obtained from dismantled aerial
bombs, to scatter around and under equipment. Fifty rocket motors
for launching 60kg general purpose bombs were located within the
24th Division perimeter at Davao.

Lt Col Julian, Lt Santilli, T/5 Harding and Pfc Hawkins, Signal,
operated in and around Davao and in the Midsayap sector. In the
latter place, pigeon communications were discovered and turned
over to the 31st Signal Company. Later, a considerable quantity
of Signal, especially radar, equipment was located. An entire
multiple transmitter installation, discovered in a cave in the Davao
area, was examined and photographed. The enemy, evidently placing
considerable importance on the destruction of this equipment, sent
back infiltration parties who were able to demolish the entire
installation.

The Signal team also collected Japanese secret documents bearing information on proposed disposition of Japanese forces in Central Mindanao in the event of an American invasion. These documents were immediately turned over to the 19th Regimental Combat Team and thence to ATIS.

By the end of June the Technical Intelligence Unit on the V-5 operation was being disbanded. Lt Col Julian returned to Eighth Army Headquarters; T/3 Simmons joined Capt Cameron from the 41st Division on Ordnance Team No. 6; Pfcs Pollack and Rosen joined Lt Bell from the Victor 2 operation and Pvt Vannucci from the Victor 1 operation and all of them transferred to X Corps Headquarters as Ordnance Team No. 6; the rest of the Technical Intelligence personnel on the Victor 5 operation, except Lt Santilli and Pfc Hawkins, returned to the Technical Intelligence Depot.

During the remaining time they served with the 24th Division, Lt Santilli and Pfc Hawkins recovered no enemy Signal dumps, though they found an appreciable quantity of Signal equipment scattered throughout the sector. Four items, including a Japanese radiosonde, were turned over to the United States troops for immediate use.

Examination of a Japanese telephone central near Davao disclosed maps and documents which were appraised with minimum delay. An accompanying map showing the wire lines of the sector was translated, together with marking tags from incoming lines.

Three radio cave installations in this area had to be walled up for tactical protection. One was inspected by Lt Santilli and Pfc Hawkins prior to its being blown up be an Intelligence and Reconnaissance squad. Japs had already burned it out and it was still partially burning when inspected. The second cave was walled up with several Japs still operating inside. The third was hastily reported with incomplete information, but was walled up before a complete survey could be made.

Upon termination of service with X Corp at the end of June, Lt Santilli and Pfc Hawkins were assigned to staff work with the Chief Signal Officer at Eighth Army. Lt Bell, Pfcs Pollack and Rosen and Pvt Vannucci, who formed Ordnance Team No. 6 with X Corps Headquarters, found that the Japanese on Mindanao had by this time little equipment. It had been withdrawn to other islands in the Philippines where United States troops had attacked and also, quantities had been depleted because of the distances involved in resupply. Consequently, little equipment of new design or with new modifications was recovered by this team.

Quantities of Japanese ammunition were destroyed by 24th Division troops because of its dangerous condition and because of the possibility of being recaptured by the enemy. However, Ordnance Team No. 6 inspected and removed for storage such ammunition as was required for tactical problems sponsored by the War and Navy Departments.

Other items recovered in this area included:

4 type 96, 25 mm single mount naval guns w/3640 rounds of shells
1 type 95, 75 mm mountain gun (inoperative) complete w/sight
28 motor vehicles (repaired and turned over to the
          Philippine Army)
2 type 10, 12 cm 45 caliber D. P. naval guns
1 Oerlikon type 20 mm shell (modified for use as a hand grenade)
1 type 99, 81 mm mortar (turned over to Eighth Army for
          training purposes)
9 weapons, various caliber, from 6.5 mm rifles to 13.2 mm
          machine cannon turned in to 310 Ordnance Company Depot)
2 types 11 and 96, 6.5 mm light machine guns
1 type 89, 50 mm grenade discharger
3 type 38, 6.5 mm rifles
1 type 89, 7.7 mm heavy machine gun
1 type 92 receiver
1 type 93, 13.2 mm machine cannon w/tripod

CHAPTER IX

THE 5250th IN MANILA

March -- September 1945

Headquarters 5250th Technical Intelligence Composite Company, Separate (Provisional) and the United States Army Technical Intelligence Depot arrived at Manila, Philippine Islands, from Finschafen, New Guinea, on 26 March 1945.

Major Manley, Commanding Officer of the Company, had preceded the organization forward, arriving in Manila 12 March to select a site for the Headquarters. Specifications for the location were that it contain housing, messing, and recreational facilities for approximately 90 officers and 185 enlisted men (72 Technical Intelligence teams), as well as shop space for analysis laboratories for each of the six services; room for the shipping and receiving department, and sufficient ground space for a motor pool and an Ordnance area for heavy equipment.

This is typical of the way in which organization locations were selected in the city of Manila after its capture: While driving about the city looking for a suitable location, Major Manley spotted two large warehouses on top of a hill, had to circle twenty-five miles around to find a bridge to cross to the area.

The place he had found turned out to be ideal. It was a 500 by 1,000 foot area (Blue print of Depot, Incl 22) four and a half miles east of downtown Manila, sufficiently removed from the dust and traffic of the destroyed city to afford privacy. Situated in San Juan Heights, a quiet residential district, the grounds were on one of the highest elevations in Manila.

The two three-story warehouses, owned by the Oriental Printing Company, were unoccupied, and adequately housed the analysis laboratories, the shipping and receiving section, the enlisted men's and certain of the officer's quarters. A private home nearby, which previously had been occuiped by a Japanese general, looked like an excellent officers club and quarters, but had already been requisitioned for a general of the United States Army. Nevertheless, everything worked out smoothly. When the general found out there would be a traffic of captured guns, tanks, and other heavy equipment being shipped in and out of the Depot close by, he relinquished the house and took another he preferred in another part of town.

The house was converted into an attractive officers club and quarters. An enlisted men's recreation club 26 x 72 feet had to be constructed, as well as showers and washing facilities for enlisted men, latrines, a garage 26 x 30 feet in the motor pool, and an outdoor theater.

With approval of the War Department, a photographic laboratory was later constructed to handle the requirements of the analysis sections and field teams. The processing of photographs taken by the 72 Technical Intelligence teams at that time assigned to the 5250th, and the preparation of the required number of copies for forwarding to the War Department, were so large a burden on existing theater facilities that they were unable to carry the load. The Technical Intelligence Photographic Laboratory became one of the largest in the theater.

Prior to completion of unloading, the ship on which Depot Headquarters had arrived was moved to another location and struck an enemy mine, damaging the hold containing much important shop equipment. This ship, carrying both records and personal gear, was not raised and some of the material salvaged until the following October.

Upon arrival at Manila, the various sections were assigned space, and commenced construction of necessary facilities. Collection and analysis were continued concurrently with construction despite the loss of the equipment from the ship. Some personnel from the analysis sections of the Depot were pooled during the major portion of May under Capt Walter Schween, who was named assistant company commander under Major Manley pending the completion of all construction projects. Lt Van Slyck, meanwhile, continued as administrative officer.

Shipping and Receiving Section

Receipts of enemy equipment at the Depot in Manila consisted of a steady flow of captured material from Technical Intelligence Field Units, from the provisional Technical Intelligence Depots in Luzon, from Headquarters Eighth Army, from Philippine bases, and from censorship detachments.

Then the laboratory work was again in full swing, arrangements were completed with Port Command for the handling of shipments of captured materiel to the United States. Standing operating procedure for the shipping of Intelligence samples, as worked out by

Major Manley in conjunction with Chiefs of Services, Headquarters, AFWESPAC, was put into effect at the Technical Intelligence Depot, and initial shipments from the Manila area to the United States were accomplished. Included in these shipments were many new types of equipment not previously analyzed as well as large shipments for training purposes.

In accordance with War Department Circular No. 13, 11 January 1945, regarding the shipment of captured material to the United States for Intelligence purposes, reports were made to the theater commander immediately upon recovery of the first, second and third item of Japanese ground force equipment not previously captured, so that this information might be cabled to Washington.

As set forth in the British-American Agreement of 15 November 1944 concerning captured Japanese Ground Forces equipment and Technical Research, shipments were also made direct to British destinations upon notification by the Director of Military Intelligence, British War Office, through the Commanding General, Army Service Forces.

Information Disseminated to Troops

Throughout this period Technical Intelligence information was disseminated to subordinate commands through the media of the "G-2 Weekly Report," edited and published by the AC of S, G-2, Sixth Army, and the "Technical Intelligence Bulletin," published by G-2, Eighth Army. Technical Intelligence units in the field had access to similar publications originating with and distributed by the various corps G-2 sections. Elaborate displays of representative articles of Japanese equipment with accompanying descriptive reading matter, were prepared by all analysis section chiefs and set up at the Technical Intelligence Depot. Later, this complete display was moved down to AFWESPAC Headquarters (pictures of this display are shown in Incl 23). A permanent display of Japanese Ordnance was also placed at Ordnance Headquarters, AFWESPAC, as requested by General Holman, Chief Ordnance Officer. AFPAC; another permanent exhibit of Japanese equipment, consisting of 33 pieces of Ordnance equipment and 17 pieces of Quartermaster equipment, was issued to the 14th AA Command for a prominent display requested by the Commanding General of the unit; and a third similar exhibit was assembled at GHQ.

Also indicative of the training aid given to troops were the thirty special Ordnance kits used during a training program instituted by Replacement Command. These kits, which were of considerable help in familiarizing the troops with Japanese infantry weapons, contained the following items:

1 - 7.7 mm heavy MG	2 - 7.7 mm rifles
1 - 7.7 mm light MG	1 - 81 mm mortar
6 - 6.5 mm rifles	1 - 50 mm mortar

Major Talcott C. Wainwright

On 20 April 1945, Major Talcott C. Wainwright who had been with the 5250th as an officer in charge both in the field and at the Medical Analysis Laboratory, died from heart attack. The success of the Technical Intelligence mission in the Pacific Theatre, particularly as pertained to the medical field, was to a great extent due to his outstanding professional knowledge and ability as a soldier.

Operations in the Philippines Begin to Close

By the end of May 1945, Technical Intelligence had secured a comprehensive and fairly detailed knowledge of all technical developments used by the enemy in the Philippine campaign. Whatever the Japanese had developed that was new in equipment and techniques had been secured, studied, analyzed -- and that information disseminated to United States troops. Quantities of enemy equipment had been captured and were being shipped to the United States for training purposes. Though the Battle of the Philippines continued and thousands of Japs still remained scattered throughout the Islands, to all intents and purposes the mission of Technical Intelligence -- that is, of the men operating directly in the field with the troops -- was drawing to a close. During the following two months, units were gradually withdrawn from the field, returned to headquarters, and staged for the Blacklist Operations.

With the "official" conclusion of the Philippine campaign in July, a survey of the results of Technical Intelligence activities from 27 March 1945, when the United States Army Technical Intelligence Depot was established in Manila, to July 1945, indicated that 952 new items of Intelligence significance had been recovered in the Philippine Islands campaign. During the same period, over 4,000 nameplates and reproductions were shipped to the Ground Industry Section, Military Intelligence Service, Washington. Also, 244 technical reports were submitted by the analysis sections of the Depot; these covered a wide variety of both new and previously reported Japanese materiel of all branches of service and were published as approved by the chiefs of services, AFWESPAC.

New Personnel Join 5250th

In June AFPAC forwarded to AFWESPAC the requirements of Sixth
Army for Technical Intelligence units for the coming operation.
Five type "A" Units, five type "B" Units, one Field Depot Unit --
a total of 52 officers and 107 enlisted men would be needed for
coming Sixth Army operations. (Page 14 of Incl 1 to Incl 24
defines composition of various units). These requirements were
incorporated in the logistical instructions issued by AFPAC.

Anticipating the Olympic and Coronet Operations on the Japanese
mainland, seventy additional officers and one hundred and twenty-
five enlisted men were requisitioned from the War Department for
Technical Intelligence duty in this theater. These figures covered only preliminary Sixth Army requirements.

The company was also augmented 1 July by the arrival from New
Guinea of Headquarters and Headquarters Detachment, 98th Quartermaster Battalion. The commanding officer, Major James D. Collie.
was made Deputy Commander of the 5250th Technical Intelligence
Company under Major Manley. The Quartermaster Battalion also
furnished office personnel during this period, and was responsible
for the company administration.

With the return of Technical Intelligence personnel to the
Depot in the ensuing months, an extensive training program as a
refresher course for this personnel and as an orientation course
for the new Technical Intelligence personnel arriving in the theater
was established at the Depot under the direction of the senior field
officer of each service. The course, based upon practical esper-
ience in the field, included lectures, charts, and a complete
display of enemy equipment. The seven-day program, which prepared
Technical Intelligence personnel for future operations, was opened
18 August with an introductory address by Major Manley and was
received with enthusiasm (schedule of classes is shown in Incl 25).
Classes were attended by all personnel present at the Depot except
those needed for section work.

The Medical, Ordnance, and Chemical Warfare analysis section
held supplementary specialist training programs for their men and
certain personnel also attended a week-long ammunition course at
LEIU No. 1.

At the end of July a request was made to GHQ that authority be granted for a Technical Intelligence pass to be authorized for issue by AFPAC to all Technical Intelligence officers operating in the Pacific theater. Authority was granted, and officers of 5250th were issued Technical Intelligence passes which considerably expedited their work.

Consolidation of All Technical Intelligence Activities Recommended

For some months past, both Col Sauve, G-2 USASOS, and Major Manley, Coordinator of Technical Intelligence, had urged the consolidation of all Technical Intelligence activities under one coordinating command at GHQ.

Shortly after the activation of United States Army Forces, Pacific, (AFPAC) they had drafted (25 May 1945) a complete plan for operation of Technical Intelligence under that headquarters and had submitted it, together with a proposed table of allotments to provide for all personnel at that time on detached service with the 5250th Technical Intelligence Company.

Assuming that a separate area command would in due course of time be formed for operations within the Philippines and southward (this came into effect 7 June when headquarters administration was changed from USASOS to United States Army Forces Western Pacific (AFWESPAC)), and pointing out that additional armies coming under AFPAC that would be totally unfamiliar with Technical Intelligence as established in SWPA, they recommended that to minimize confusion delay and duplication of effort, centralized control under AFPAC be established.

Their recommendation was temporarily shelved but was later adopted on an even more comprehensive scale. When the atomic bomb suddenly emerged upon the scene, when the war was abruptly ended, and the entire industrial, scientific and technological resources of the Japanese Empire were opened for investigation, centralized control - not only for the United States Army but for all Allied Headquarters - was mandatory.

End of the War

Friday evening, 10 August 1945, around 2100 hours, the Manila radio station, KZT, broadcast that it had been "unofficially" announced that the Japanese Imperial Government had indicated they would accept the Potsdam peace terms. After the long wait Saturday night, 11 August, the news of the Japanese surrender was officially confirmed in Manila Sunday morning, 12 August.

Every plan that had been made for the impending Olympic Operation was suspended. The Armies made a rapid shift of weight from combat force to army of occupation.

Technical Intelligence Units were alerted to move to Japan 23 August, necessitating an immediate and tremendous turnover of personnel. Practically all personnel in the field were ordered immediately into the United States Army Technical Intelligence Depot. At the same time, arrangements were made to attach additional personnel to the 5250th so that more teams could be organized. Thirty-eight new officers and 58 enlisted men from all branches of service joined the organization during the course of the month.

All Technical Intelligence units were equipped and trained and ready to move out on the dates set by General Headquarters.

Major construction projects finished during August were new enlisted men and officer mess halls and two buildings originally intended for the Medical analysis section. Crowded conditions in the enlisted men's and officers' quarters caused by the additional personnel reporting in from the field were alleviated by moving approximately 50 enlisted men into the section which formerly served as a mess hall and by using the Medical analysis building as additional officers quarters. With the sudden move to Japan, the enlarged Medical laboratory was not needed, and construction of a storage warehouse for the Signal analysis section was delayed pending decision on the future status of the United States Army Technical Intelligence Depot in the Philippine sector. The movement of a majority of field units to line organizations eliminated quartering of personnel as a problem by the end of August.

Preliminary plans for coordination of scientific investigations and Technical Intelligence in connection with ultimate operations were discussed at a conference held early in the month with the Special Scientific Consultant from the War Department, the Pacific Warfare Board, and the Office of the Counter-Intelligence, GHQ.

The recommendation that had been made earlier in May by Col Sauve and Lt Col Manley(recently promoted) to G-2, General Headquarters that the 5250th Technical Intelligence Composite Company, Separate (Provisional), at that time under the control of AFWESPAC should be attached to GHQ for operational control, again came to the fore.

A recommendation from Chief Engineer, GHQ, to G-2, GHQ, advising the same set-up, kept the matter open, and at another conference, with G-2 and Chief Engineer, GHQ, in the latter part of August, it became increasingly evident that Technical Intelligence would be able to operate much more effectively out of higher headquaters. It was decided that no action could be taken immediately but that GHQ would arrive at a definite decision in the matter.

Little was done about Japanese material in the Philippines at this time, as it was anticipated that all requirements could be met more satisfactorily in Japan and that the problem of Japanese material in the AFWESPAC area would be one of local disposition.

Few bookings were placed with Port Command because of a tendency of services involved to stop all shipments until clarification from Washington of material required, due to the change caused by the surrender of Japan.

Lt Col Manley submitted to G-2, GHQ, a draft of recommended regulations to supercede USAFFE Circular 83, 1944, on the disposition of captured enemy material in the Pacific theater, The draft contained a recommendation for retention of various items as souvenirs by individual soldiers since hostilities had been terminated.

T. I. Personnel Depart for Occupation of Japan

Personnel from ten Field Units and Field Depot Unit were assigned from 5250th to Sixth and Eighth Armies during August as part of the occupation forces for Japan (Blacklist operation) This split between both Armies the T.I. units originally intended for Sixth Army alone.

Five type "A" Units were formed and placed on orders as follows:

Field Unit No. 1, Hq Sixth Army (departed Manila 4 Sep 45)
Field Unit No. 2, X Corps, Sixth Army (departed Manila 20 Sep 45)
Field Unit No. 3, I Corps, Sixth Army ("   "   28 Aug 45)
Field Unit No. 4, XI Corps, Eighth Army ("   "   28 Aug 45)
Field Unit No. 5, XIV Corps, Eighth Army ("   "   25 Aug 45)

Field Depot Unit No. 71 was created and assigned to Sixth Army Headquarters, departing Manila 4 September 1945.

Five type "B" Units were formed and placed on orders:

Field Unit No. 51, I Corps, Sixth Army (departed Manila 29 Aug 45)
Field Unit No. 52, I Corps, Sixth Army ("   "   30 Aug 45)
Field Unit No. 53, XI Corps, Eighth Army ("   "   28 Aug 45)
Field Unit No. 54, XIV Corps, Eighty Army ("   "   25 Aug 45)
Field Unit No. 55, IX Corps, Eighth Army ("   "   24 Aug 45)

(A roster of personnel of these field units comprising a total of 53 officers and 100 enlisted men, is shown in Incl 3).

Technical Intelligence target objective folders were published and distributed to the Units as they left the Depot as well as to all corps and divisions under Sixth Army. These folders outlined by areas various targets of interest to Technical and Technological Intelligence on the Islands of Japan. Forms for reporting on Japanese industrial installations were also distributed to the teams.

Upon the departure of Major Collie and Lt Van Slyck on operations, Capt William G. Shaw III was appointed executive officer of the 5250th. 1st Lt Herbert J. Jubelirer (later promoted to Captain) was appointed supply officer, and 1st Lt Edwin Kurtz was appointed assistant administrative and mess officer. Lt Col Erwin E. Sullo reported early in September to take charge of the Signal Analysis Section; he was also elected president of the officers club upon the departure of Major Harry E. Carnes to the United States.

Equipment and Information

With the war ended, the quantity of new captured enemy equipment received at the Depot during the month was negligible. Analysis of enemy equipment at the Manila depot had ceased by September, except for clearing up 58 reports already under way.

All equipment on hand was disposed of as soon as possible.
In the month of August 194,080 pounds of enemy material were
shipped to the United States by water; 2,020 pounds by air;
and 150 pounds by Army courier service.   Water bookings
during the same period amounts to 97,850 pounds. Air shipment of enemy Ordnance material to Military Intelligence Service,(MIS)
United States Army Forces European Theater, Paris, France, left
Manila 5 August. Two hundred twenty-eight photographs of capture
enemy material were forwarded to Map and Photo Division, (MIS),
Washington, D. C., and 283 nameplates and miscellaneous rubbings
were sent to Ground Industry Section, MIS, during the same period.

Twenty-one copies of compilation on Japanese economic data from
the Signal Section were submitted to the Office of the Assistant
Chief of Staff, G-2, AFWESPAC, for further distribution to Sixth
and Eighth Armies, and additions to the Japanese Chemical Warfare
Notebook were sent to the printers.

Ordnance materiel which had been captured aboard the Japanese
hospital ship "Tachibana Maru" was turned over to the United States
Army Technical Intelligence Depot to be inventoried, photographed,
reported, and retained in storage with its original packaging,
pending receipt of instructions from the Commander-in-Chief, Army
Forces Pacific.   It was held for use by the War Crimes Branch,
AFPAC, in possible war crimes trials.   Troops that had seized
the hospital ship, however, had been allowed to souvenir much
of the equipment before Technical Intelligence was notified.
Equipment salvaged (photographs, Incl 26) includes:

       27 bayonets
       56 type 89 50 mm grenade dischargers
       1 type 10 50 mm flare discharger
       257 type 38 6.5 mm rifles
       2 type 93 field light range finders
       1 type 93 triped bar light range finders
       4 type 92 70 mm battalion guns (incomplete)
       13 mounts for heavy machine guns
       22 spare barrels for heavy machine guns
       4 range drums for 70 mm battalion guns
       35 type 96 6.5 mm light machine guns
       73 magazines for light machine guns
       4 clip loaders
       62 spare barrels for light machine guns
       14 type 92 7.7 mm heavy machine guns
       9 anti-aircraft adapters

This Ordnance materiel was packed and marked as enemy Medical
equipment with packages and boxes marked with large Red Crosses.
The 70 mm battalion guns were disassembled and packed in boxes
bearing the Red Cross. The rifles were packed in straw matting
bundles containing from four to ten rifles with each bundle labeled
with a Red Cross.

5250th Ordered to Tokyo

In submitting a report (17 September 1945) on the disposition
of personnel present with the 5250th Technical Intelligence Company
available for the occupation of Japan, Col Sauve' and Lt Col Manley
again urged the centralization of Technical Intelligence administration
under General Headquarters (Incl 27).

Subsequently, a series of conferences were held with Col Walter
S. Wood, G-2 Section, GHQ, relative to the transfer of the 5250th for
direct administration under GHQ. Recommendations included proposed
directive to be issued by GHQ when that headquarters should assume
direct responsibility for Technical Intelligence in the Pacific theater.
Col Wood left shortly thereafter for General Headquarters Advance in
Japan. Final approval for reassignment of the 5250th Technical Intelligence Company to GHQ and coordination of all scientific, technical,
and technological Intelligence under GHQ was given by Lt General R.K.
Sutherland Chief of Staff GHQ AFPAC (GO 337 & 369, H2, 20 and 30
November 1945 Incl 28 and 29).

Col Wood was appointed Coordinator of War Department Intelligence
Targets (WDIT) under Major General Charles A. Willoughby, G-2, AFPAC;
Lt Col David S. Tait was appointed Coordinator of all Technical Intelligence; and Lt Col Manley continued as Commanding Officer of the
5250th Technical Intelligence Company, which, in addition to its normal
functions, was to be responsible for the United States Army Technical
Intelligence Center under G-2, GHQ, SCAI. The Technical Intelligence
Center was to provide housing, messing and recreation accommodations
for officer, enlisted, civilian, and visiting foreign personnel for
all Technical Intelligence within the theater.

Action was taken to close down the United States Army Technical
Intelligence Depot, Manila, and to transfer it, together with the
5250th Technical Intelligence Company, to Tokyo. No new analysis of
enemy equipment was undertaken. No new equipment was shipped in from
the field. All personnel remaining in the field reported in to the
Depot. All salvage materiel was disposed of in accordance with theater
policy. All enemy equipment on hand was shipped to the United States.
Accounts of Shipping and Receiving were closed 10 October 1945.

New adjusted service ratings as of 2 September 1945 were turned in to Headquarters, AFWESPAC, and shortly thereafter men from the Company eligible for release from the Army under the point system were returned to the United States. Additional personnel required to take their place with the organization were requisitioned. (Dates of joining and departing from the organization for all personnel of 5250th are included in Incl 9.)

In October, per verbal orders of Lt Col Manley, all analysis sections of the Depot were closed and prepared for shipment. Depot headquarters, mess, supply, and shipping and receiving section remained open until just before the company departed.

On 15 October Lt Col Manley was sent to Tokyo to make necessary arrangements for the movement of the 5250th Technical Intelligence Company to Japan.

On 18 October movement orders were sent by radiogram from GHQ AFPAC, ADVANCE (in Tokyo), directing that the organization be moved with ATIS from Manila to Tokyo, with 60 days rations and organic transportation. (Incl 29).

Authority for movement having been obtained, supplies were drawn, a meeting of officers was held, instructions were received, and personnel were alerted.

On 6 November 33 officers of the 5250th left for Tokyo on the ship, "Kinkad" and on 9 November the balance of the personnel of the 5250th Technical Intelligence Company moved with all organic equipment on the "Francis Ogden" -- time of arrival in Tokyo, 20 November 1945.

HISTORY OF TECHNICAL INTELLIGENCE

C H A P T E R X

TECHNICAL INTELLIGENCE CENTER: JAPAN

October -- November 1945

Lt Col Manley had flown to Tokyo before the 5250th Technical
Intelligence Company sailed from Manila, to make preliminary
arrangements for the transfer of the unit to Japan.

G-2, GHQ, directed that a United States Army Technical
Intelligence Center be established at Tokyo Arsenal No. 1,
Shimojujo, Ojaka, Tokyo. The Center was to be administered
by the 5250th Technical Intelligence Company with Lt Col Manley
as Commanding Officer.

The Imperial Japanese Government was notified through the
Central Liaison Office, Tokyo (memorandum AG 601 (19 Oct 45)
GD, Subject: Acquisition of Certain Facilities of Tokyo Arsenal
No. 1, dated 19 October 1945) that buildings 255, 263, 269, 276,
395, 475, 481 and the open areas adjacent to these buildings of
the Arsenal would be "made available immediately for occupancy by
an agency of General Headquarters of the Supreme Commander for
the Allied Powers" (GH 2, SCAI).

The Imperial Japanese Government was directed that all
items of supplies, equipment, furniture, furnishings and fix-
tures would remain in the buildings until a representative of
General Headquarters of the Supreme Commander for the Allied
Powers designated the items required for use by the Allied
Forces and those items which might be removed.

It was further directed that the Imperial Japanese Government make necessary arrangements to have a representative of their
office at building 395 at 1000, 20 October 1945, for a meeting
with the representative of General Headquarters of the Supreme
Commander for the Allied Powers. The details pertaining to the
work to be accomplished and the installation of the facilities
referred to above would be "communicated to your representative
at that time".

Lt Col Manley met with the Japanese representatives at the
Arsenal 20 October and directed them as to the installation of
bathing, sanitary, messing and other facilities which would be
required and directed that buildings and grounds requisitioned

would be thoroughly cleaned prior to occupancy by the 5250th
Technical Intelligence Company.

Description of the Arsenal

The portion of Tokyo Arsenal No. 1 turned over for use as
the United States Army Technical Intelligence Center, comprised
eight buildings (Pictures and Blueprints of Depot, Incls 28 and
29) with a total of 157,949 square feet floor space, and a ground
area 1000 by 1500 feet square.

The main building, which had formerly been used as the administration center for the Tokyo Arsenal, was taken over for administration headquarters for the 5250th. One 3-story building was
used for the shipping and receiving section, for company supply,
and for the combined Army-Navy library of the Washington Document
Center, Advance. One 2-story building was converted into laboratories and offices for the six analysis sections of the Company.

One building, part of which was 5 stories high, was used
for mess hall, quarters, and recreation center for officers, and
a similar building was designated for similar use for enlisted
men. A large warehouse was utilized as garage and motor pool,
where all vehicles could be stored indoors. The seventh building
was a theater for company personnel. Another building, which
housed two scientific laboratories with testing equipment intact,
was taken over in addition to the seven previously requisitioned
and was available for use by technical personnel for analysis of
Intelligence samples of Japanese materiel.

Transfer of the 5250th to GHQ

Upon his return to Manila, Lt Col Manley appointed Lt Col
Sullo, Majors Madigan and Hirst, and Capt Shaw as forward echelon to fly to Tokyo to complete arrangements for the arrival
of the Company. They arrived 26 October supervised the clearance
of the buildings and had the premises set up so that when the
ships with the balance of the Company aboard docked in Tokyo
Bay the Arsenal was ready for occupancy.

After the Company sailed from Manila, Lt Col Manley flew
to Tokyo, leaving Capt Mary A. Chave, Assistant Coordinator of
Technical Intelligence, and Lt Edwin A. Kurtz, Assistant Administrative Officer, as rear echelon for the organization. They
followed 22 November.

In a conference with G-1, G-2, and G-3, GHQ, in regard to
the transfer of the Technical Intelligence Company from AFWESPAC
to GHQ, it had been recommended that the personnel be assigned to

GHQ, Special Troops, and it was suggested as desirable to preserve the entity of the organization in its name, "5250th", the number assigned it under the orders establishing the organization as a "Separate, (Provisional)" Company under USASOS.

AFPAC assigned the company to Special Troops, General Headquarters, Supreme Command for the Allied Powers, upon their departure from Manila. General Orders 337, General Headquarters, Army Forces Pacific, dated 20 November 1945, established the 5250th Technical Intelligence Company as a theater overhead installation and stated that grades and ratings would be authorized by separate communication. General Order 369, same headquarters, dated 30 Nov 45, dissolved the 5250th Technical Intelligence Composite Company, Separate (Provisional).

By letter order AG 320.3 (20 Nov 45) GA, General Headquarters, United States Army Forces, Pacific, Subject: Allotment of Theater Overhead Grades and Strength, dated 29 November 1945, allotment of theater overhead grades and ratings was made to the 5250th Technical Intelligence Company as follows:

Officers:

Col	Lt Col	Major	Capt	1st Lt	2d Lt	Total
1	3	10	23	40	13	90

Warrant Officers:

CWO: 1		1

Enlisted Men (grades as shown):

1st	2d	3d	4th	5th	6th	7th	
1	12	17	35	46	48	10	170

Aggregate 261

Occupation Instructions No. 2

Occupation Instructions No. 2, Office of the Supreme Commander for the Allied Powers, dated 25 September 1945, outlined to the occupation forces for Japan the general instructions governing the collection and disposition of enemy equipment of the Japanese armed forces. This was the broad outline. The disposition of enemy equipment collected for Intelligence purposes was governed by later directives.

HISTORY OF TECHNICAL INTELLIGENCE

General Orders No. 9

General Orders No. 9, General Headquarters, Supreme Commander for the Allied Powers, Subject: Japanese Military Intelligence Targets, dated 2 October 1945 (Incl 32) designated the Assistant Chief of Staff, G-2, GHQ, to coordinate and supervise the exploitation of military intelligence targets in Japan and Korea.

Under this General Order, the exploitation of targets and objectives included coordination and utilization of certain general and technical Intelligence agencies: the 5250th Technical Intelligence Company, including the United States Army Technical Intelligence Depot and field unit personnel; Translator Interpreter Service (TIS, a revised ATIS organization) Combined Document Center and field detachments; special staff sections responsible for the technical supervision of their respective Technical sections in the 5250th, including laboratory and field teams; Air Corps and Navy technical units analogous to the 5250th Technical Intelligence Company; and special technical missions, national and foreign.

Coordinating control and supervision over the various agencies interested in Technical Intelligence investigations were exercised through normal command and staff channels. These agencies included special staff sections of AFPAC Armies, separate Corps, Commander in Chief of the Pacific, Far Eastern Air Forces, United States Army Strategic Air Force, Allied agencies, and special missions represented in Japan and Korea. Each of these agencies designated plenary representatives to the Assistant Chief of Staff, G-2, GHQ, who operated under his control and whose mission was to coordinate and supervise Technical Intelligence activities to prevent competitive duplication of effort.

Technical Intelligence in the Pacific theater was designed to accomplish the following objectives: First, the exploitation of materiel, including the examination and evaluation of available enemy materiel and deduction, from this evaluation, of the state of Japanese resources for war. Intelligence so obtained was exploited for the reciprocal benefit of the United States and Allied Armed Forces. This included examination of Japanese facilities which might be involved in the production of materiel for war and the provision of trained personnel to assist the chiefs of services (Ground, Naval and Air) in the supervision of the collection, safeguarding and evacuation of captured enemy equipment for Intelligence study and for tactical and training purposes.

Second objective of Technical Intelligence in the Pacific was the exploitation of documents. This involved providing trained personnel to screen and inventory enemy documents; circulating accession results, that is lists of documents received, to authorized agencies; extracting Intelligence needed for security and control by means of fragmentary translations or photostats; selecting military, technical, scientific and general documents for transmission to the United States pertaining to current target books published by the War and Navy Departments and the specific interests of specialist agencies; and, finally, focusing all field agencies of the Ground, Naval and Air Forces through TIS for document activity.

Third objective of Technical Intelligence was the exploitation of Order of Battle Intelligence and related subjects: this involved lists of all regular units (Ground, Naval and Air) lists of code names and numbers, T/O's and T/E's of all types of units; lists of divisions, brigades and major units of Ground, Naval and Air Forces by components, strength, armament, etc; lists of recruiting districts and units trained therein; lists of Army and Navy officers and their commands, including directories of transfers and promotions, biographies and service records; histories of major units; investigations of recruiting and training systems, of Home Guard and Volunteer Defense Units; investigations of military police, together with records of special and secret service organizations, (Tokumu Kikan); investigations of military intelligence agencies, including histories, operations, etc; and, finally, reports on military societies.

Fourth objective of Technical Intelligence was exploitation of historical records and official reports of the Japanese General Staff (Ground, Naval and Air). This included the organization of Japan for war, the preparations for the War of 1941, compaigns in the Southwest Pacific Area from 1942 to 1944, campaigns in the Philippines from 1941 to 1942, second campaign in the Philippines in 1945, campaigns in the Pacific islands from 1941 to 1945, and campaigns in other areas from 1941 to 1945.

For effective coordination, the following policy provisions were enforced:

To prevent competitive duplication, all foreign and national technical missions upon arrival were registered with the Assistant Chief of Staff, G-2, GHQ, who notified the occupation authorities concerned; G-2, GHQ, conducted all liaison with the Japanese Governmental authorities relative to the operation of technical missions, delegating such liaison as was required to occupation force commanders; since Intelligence targets were geographically distributed, the occupation force commanders were responsible for the coordination

of exploitation of targets within their territorial jurisdiction,
operating through subordinate commanders or staffs to prevent competitive duplications. To expedite the conduct of these investigations,
G-2, GHQ, was authorized to correspond directly with the heads of the
various interested agencies previously mentioned or their representatives on technical details, and direct correspondence between plenary
representatives and the heads of the agencies they represented was
authorized. To protect Intelligence materiel and records available in
only limited numbers against exploitation by a single research agency
and to make these items accessible to other Intelligence agencies their
removal had to be cleared through the occupation force commander.
The principle of reciprocal exchange of reports applying to all field
technical agencies, all reports of Technical Intelligence relating to
investigations in Japan and Korea were cleared through the Assistant
Chief of Staff, G-2, GHQ, prior to their being dispatched to locations
outside the area.

War Department Intelligence Target Section

     The War Department Intelligence Target Section (WDIT) was
established under the provisions of General Orders No.9, 2 October
1945 and General Orders No.15, 9 November 1945, to exercise coordinating control and supervision over the exploitation of military and
civilian Intelligence targets of interdepartmental and international
concern in Japan and Korea.

     Col Walter S. Wood, appointed chief of WDIT, coordinated, super-
vised and established policy for the activities of the technical,
civilian and military subsections of WDIT and their relations with
all other agencies.

     Operating under Col Wood, was the Technical Intelligence Section,
headed by Lt Col David S. Tait, which was responsible for Technical
Intelligence of all descriptions in the Pacific Theater. This section
coordinated the activities of the Chiefs of Services of AFPAC, the
U.S. Special Technical Missions, the Foreign Technical Missions, made
arrangements concerning the exploitation of targets of Technical
Intelligence interest, and saw that proper technical personnel were
assigned to complete the reports.

     Operating within the Technical Intelligence Section were: U.S.
Army Technical Intelligence Center (5250th Technical Intelligence Co.);
Collection and Reports Sub-Section, which coordinated the reports submitted with War and Navy Department Intelligence targets; Translator
& Interpreter Service (2,000 personnel), charged with the translation
and publication of all Japanese documents and with the furnishing of
translator and interpreter personnel; Washington Document Center

(ADVON) which selected and shipped all Japanese documents to the United States; and War Department Intelligence Collection Committ (ADVON), created by the Joint Chiefs of Staffs, which advised the Theater concerning the transmittal to Washington of Intelligence information.

Included in the U.S. and Foreign Technical Missions coordinated under the Technical Intelligence Section were the following agencies: Naval Technical Mission to Japan, Economic and Scientific Section, British Staff Section, United States Strategic Bomb Survey, Japanese Antiaircraft and Seacoast Artillery Research Board, Air Technical Intelligence Group (Far Eastern Air Forces), British Amphibious Mission, U.S. Naval Shipping Control Authority for Japanese Merchant Marine and Austrialian Scientific Mission.

—   Temporary passes from the Office of the Supreme Commander for the Allied Powers, Military Intelligence Section, were issued to authorized personnel in accordance with provisions of General Order No.9 to permit the bearer to enter any restricted area in Japan or Korea South of 38 degrees north latitude for purposes of Technical Intelligence.

Agencies furnished weekly a list of targets to be visited, notifying WDIT at least 48 hours in advance so that the local commander of the area and Translator and Interpreter Service could be notified.

All requests on the Japanese Government were funneled through WDIT.

Upon completion of target investigation, report was submitted to WDIT.

Technical Intelligence Instruction No.1

Lt Col Tait, when he was assigned at GHQ, AFPAC, in Manila, had strongly favored coordination of Technical Intelligence when Col Sauve and Lt Col Manley had first proposed it in writing in May 1945. As Coordinator of Technical Intelligence under Col Wood at Tokyo, Lt Col Tait drew up Technical Intelligence Instruction No.1, General Headquarters. Military Intelligence Section, General Staff, dated 20 November 1945, that laid the foundation for the coordination of all Technical Intelligence activities relative to the occupation of Japan.

Under this directive, the following policies prevailed:

The United States Army Technical Intelligence Center served as
headquarters for the 5250th Technical Intelligence Company. As field
units of the 5250th completed their work with Armies, Corps and
Divisions, they were recalled to the Center for re-assignment under
G-2. Special investigators temporarily attached to chiefs of services
and other agencies could also be assigned to the organization for
administration while in the theater.

Chiefs of services and other Intelligence agencies prepared
plans for the exploitation of military Intelligence targets in their
designated fields and filed these plans with G-2 for coordination
with other agencies at least 48 hours in advance of execution.
The plans listed the names of personnel involved, stated the
transportation and equipment required, and presented a brief outline
of contemplated procedure.

To assist in the investigations, additional qualified personnel,
as well as transportation and equipment, could be requested from the
5250th through G-2 Operations (Major Henry W. Hall) on WDIT Form No.1.
Photographers from the Photograph Laboratry that had been established
at the Technical Intelligence Depot in Manila and reestablished at the
Technical Intelligence Center in Tokyo, could also be requested to
accompany investigators on field trips.

G-2 assumed responsibility for notifying other interested
agencies; arranged with the occupation forces the details of billeting
and transportation; notified, through its Japanese Liaison Section, the
Japanese authorities involved; and, when desired, arranged for prr-
liminary interviews with Japanese officials that often materially
expedited the investigations.

All interested agencies maintained a close liaison with G-2 and
were held responsible for becoming familiar with the records and
reports of Intelligence investigation maintained in the Technical
Intelligence Subsection of WDIT so that unnecessary duplication of
effort could be avoided.

—   Documents necessary to complete investigations were evacuated
through TIS to the Washington Document Center (Advance) Library at
the Technical Intelligence Center.

Samples of new or modified material or equipment which was to
be evacuated were handled as follows: When practicable, the investigator personally evacuated the item to the Technical Intelligence
Center. If this were not adviseable, he made arrangements with
Division G-2 for packing and shipping the equipment, and notified the
Technical Intelligence Center that it had been sent. If shipment were
delayed, he notified the Division G-2, who was responsible for safe-

guarding it until such time as the appropriate agency could arrange shipment to the Technical Intelligence Center, where further study of the material could be made at one of the analysis laboratories. If shipment were inadvisable, the investigator completed such study and photographs as were necessary and arranged with the Division G-2 for the security of the item. In all cases, final disposition was requested from the War Department and effected by Technical Intelligence Center personnel.

Upon completion of the investigation, it was necessary that a report be submitted. To insure its adequacy, the Chief of Service specifically indicated in his orders to the investigating personnel the questions he desired answered. The report was mimeographed and distributed by the Technical Intelligence Center.

Activities of Technical Intelligence Teams in the Field

At the time of concluding the writing of this history of Technical Intelligence, not all reports of the teams in the field had been received at 5250th Headquarters. Those available, however, indicate the conditions encountered in Japan, the cooperation that was given by the conquered people, the jobs that were assigned Technical Intelligence teams in the occupied country, and the type of information that could be secured.

Assigned to Sixth Army were the followig Technical Intelligence units (personnel are included in operations roster, Incl 3):

              Field Unit No.1............Headquarters, Sixth Army
              Field Unit No.2............X Corps
              Field Unit No.3............I Corps
              Field Unit No.51...........I Corps
              Field Unit No.52...........I Corps
              Field Depot Unit No.71.....Headquarters, Sixth Army

Field Unit No.1 Headquarters Sixth Army

Field Unit No.1 was assigned to Headquarters, Sixth Army, where they investigated the Civilian Defense Corps at Tsuruga, Fukui Prefecture, on the northern coast of Honshu. Investigation showed that the Corps, which was organized along lines similar to many agencies in the United States, apparently was not successful in accomplishing its mission due to a lack of facilities, equipment and management.

HISTORY OF TECHNICAL INTELLIGENCE

Hiroshima and Kure, Honshu, Japan

Field Unit No.2 was placed on temporary duty with X Corps, and assigned VOCG on operations with the 41st Infantry Division. Since the Unit was only allowed two jeeps in the first echelon of X Corps, 1st Lt Cyril L. Martin, Medical officer for the unit, was left in charge of a detail to bring up a $\frac{1}{4}$-ton truck and trailer with the second echelon. The other men from the Unit remaining behind with him on Mindanao, Philippine Islands, were: Cpl Robert E. Jones, CWS; Pfc Rudy G. Colby, CE; T/5 Nick P. Vannucci, Ord; and T/4 Estill C. Picklesimer, Signal Corps.

The first echelon arrived at Hiro, Honshu, Japan, 7 October 1945, with specific targets accessible, Army Ordnance Supply Depot at Hiroshima and Kure Naval Base and Ordnance Arsenal at Kure (Map Incl. 33). The branch office of the Tokyo Electric Company was not located and was believed to have been destroyed by bombing, and six other targets listed for investigation also could not be located. Police and Japanese officials stated they had not heard of any of these installations in Hiroshima.

2d Lt Robert E. Cleary, Jr., and Pfc Ralph H. Spevack of the Chemical Warfare Team of this unit, recovered a new type decontaminator for dry mix in the Hiroshima Army Ordnance Depot.

Major William O. Farnam, Jr., and T/5 William C. Carrett, Engineer Team, recovered a new item, a small jack hammer, which was reported and returned to the Technical Intelligence Center. As requested by 41st Infantry Division, this searched several caves near Kure, but no items of Technical Intelligence value were recovered.

Capt Edward Nowakowski and T/5 Kenneth I. Moore, Ordnance, checked the caves near Kure with the Engineer Team, but also failed to recover any equipment of Intelligence value. At the Kure Naval Arsenal a new mobile 20 cm rocket launcher was recovered. At the Hiroshima Army Ordnance Supply Depot, new items found included: 15 cm horse-drawn mortar; 37 mm anti-tank gun (the gun was on a mount similar to type 1, 47 mm AT gun); and an amphibious tank (destroyed), which the Japanese claimed was the only one existing in Japan (manufacturer unknown, but tank was made in Sagami, near Tokyo). Quantities of items contained in another target were received from the 41st Division.

2d Lt Anthony G. Coppola and S/Sgt William J. Poss, Quartermaster Team, recovered a Japanese potato peeling machine in working condition at officers quarters, Kure.

1st Lt William F. Howland and T/4 Albert J. Kaplan, Signal Corps, found small quantities of Army Signal equipment at Hiroshima, but they were of no value because of deliberate smashing.

As a whole, little equipment was found by members of Field Unit No. 2. Limited transportation and washed out roads contributed to the meager results, and the primary value was that Hiroshima had been almost completely wiped off the map in the atomic bombing raid.

I Corps Sector in Japan

Field Units 3, 51 and 52 operated with I Corps in the South-Central Honshu area. Field Unit No. 3, on temporary duty to the 25th Infantry Division, spent September awaiting shipment to the Nagoya sector (Map Incl 33). They arrived late that month, after being delayed some 20 days due to weather and mines in the Nagoya harbor. The volume of work was heavy, but the unit attempted to visit all targets of importance before the Division destruction teams destroyed the equipment.

CWS Team No. 3, (1st Lt Charles F. Melchor, Jr., Sgt Carl H. Johnson, Pvt Charles W. Poth) investigated all Chemical Warfare targets listed for the Nagoya area. Information was obtained in each case from detailed interrogation through Japanese interpreters of factory managers and from physical inspections of the factories. A list of targets investigated and information obtained therefrom was as follows:

Nissan Chemical Plant, located in the dock area of Nagoya, was found to be a branch plant of the Nissan Chemical Industrial Co., Ltd., with main officers in Tokyo. War production consisted of bulk manufacture of fuming sulphuric acid and super phosphate. No chemical research was carried on at this plant, and standard methods of industrial synthesis were used. The plant was only slightly damaged during hostilities and at the time of investigation was continuing operation for the production of sulphuric acid.

Tokai Soda Company was formerly located adjacent to the Nissan Chemical Plant, but had been totally destroyed during hostilities. No further information concerning this plant could be obtained.

Tokai Sodium Co., through listed as a target on available maps of Nagoya in the vicinity of Nissan Chemical Plant, was reported by Nissan plant officials who were interrogated to have moved to another part of Japan prior to hostilities. A search of the surrounding area apparently confirmed this report.

Yahagi Electro-Chemical Plant and Showa Soda Plant, located in the dock area of Nagoya, combined during hostilities under joint management for the production of bulk chemicals. Standard processes were used for the manufacture of all chemicals and no apparent chemical research had been or was being conducted. With very little plant damage sustained during hostilities, production was being continued.

Sakura Gum Co., Ltd., Nagoya Branch (formerly Dai Nippon Cellophane Plant), was located north of Nagoya Castle, Nagoya. Wartime products were rubber tubes for airplane gasoline hose, rubber tubing for airplane high pressure hydraulic hose, and sheet cellophane. Equipment from the section which manufactured rubber tubes had been moved to other plants. The cellophane plant, which was destroyed by bombing, was rebuilt and resumed the manufacture of cellophane around 1 December 1945.

In summary, it was apparent that these large chemical industial plants were engaged only in the manufacture of intermediate products and not in the production of finished war materiel, which was accomplished in other plants. Evidently these plants were not charged with the responsibility of chemical research, since the only laboratories encountered were for production control. The primary responsibility of these plants in wartime seemed to be quantity production of essentially the same chemicals which had been produced in peacetime.

Only one member of Engineer Team No.3 was still assigned to field duty by 9 November. The other two members, 2d Lt Wendell S. Webster and T/3 Arnold F. Wellensiek, had been relieved of duty with T.I. Unit No.3 and had been assigned to the 11th Replacement Depot for return to the United States.

Only member of the Medical Team left by the middle of November was 1st Lt Henry T. Zelechosky. Pfc Ira A Davidson of this team had transferred to the 11th Replacement Depot for return to the United States.

Capt Robert L. Henry, Jr., reported to the Replacement Depot, leaving T/4 Robert W. Grubbs and Pfc Joseph F. Pollack without an officer in charge of the Ordnance Team.

1st Lt Philip C. Anderson, upon the departure of T/5 John M. Devlin for the Replacement Depot, continued as the only member of the Quartermaster Team. He also acted as officer in charge of the Field Unit.

The Signal Team (2d Lt John H. Lotz, S/Sgt Max A. Bratt, (who reported to the Replacement Depot 17 November, and S/Sgt Robert H. Groom) covered the Nagoya Aircraft Plotting Center, made a complete

inventory of all Japanese Signal targets listed in target folder
for the 25th Infantry Division area, and shipped important items
to the Technical Intelligence Center, Tokyo.

Investigation at Kobe, Honshu.

Field Unit No.51, on temporary duty to 33rd Infantry Division
of I Corps, arrived in Kobe, Honshu, (Map Incl 33) 25 September.
The first impression was that Kobe was completely ruined, but later
more thorough inspections led to the recovery of considerable information and materiel.

The CWS Team composed of 2d Lt Robert C. Payant, Sgt Harvey J.
Bylsma, and Cpl Homer Blankenship, investigated the Cavalry School
dump at Himeji (Map, Incl 33), and recovered the following items in
the quantities indicated:

    3 boxes .....HCN frangible smoke grenades
16 boxes......type 94 substitute smoke candles
10 boxes......type 94 small smoke candles (A)
  8 boxes......type 94 floating smoke candles (B)
20 boxes......50 mm smoke shells for type 89 grenade discharger
10 boxes......frangible vomiting gas grenades
10 boxes......colored smoke candles
30...........type 91 Army gas masks

Other targets investigated by this team included: Nisshin
Milling Co.,Ltd., Kobe; Nagaoka Kuchugai Manufacturing Company, Kobe;
Nippin Dunlop Rubber Company, Kobe; Sanyo Chemical Factory, Himeji;
Himeji Cavalry School, Himeji; Kobe Port Defense Garrison, Kobe;
Mitsui Warehouse No. 324, Kobe; Koyosed Factory, Takarazuka (Map,
Incl 33), National Bearing Works, Takarazuka; Japanese Himeji Army
Disciplinary Barracks, Himeji.

The Engineer Team, composed of Capt William C. Gohring, T/4
Alvin J. Orville, and Pvt James W. Stephen, found no Engineer equipment,
with the exception of small hand tools located at the 4th Infantry Replacement Unit, Osaka Division, Himeji, Japan.

This same team, investigating the Kobe Shipbuilding Plant of
Mitsubishi, Heavy Industries, Ltd. 3 Chome Wadasakicho Hyogoku, Kobe,
Honshu, found the plant had not been damaged during the war and was
at the time of investigation capable of full production. The plant's
main production during war and peace time had been shipbuilding and

the fabrication of steel and iron pipes and railroad rails.
Operations at the plant at the time of report consisted of minor
repairs on six merchant cargo ships of from 850 to 6800 gross tons.

Other targets investigated by this team were: Osakokikoi,
Seisakusho; Amagasaki, Seikosho KK; Nichio Seiko KK; Sumitomo Zinzoku
Kogyo KK; Oriental Steamship Company; Tao Kinzuko Togyo KK; Tokyo
Electric Company; Kobe Shipbuilding Plant; 4th Infantry Replacement
Unit.

The Ordnance Team was composed of Capt Nelson J. Sweet, officer
in charge of the entire unit, T/5 Richard E. Reynolds, and Pfc.
James E. Unruh. With the initial impression that Kobe was completely
ruined and that factory targets were nil, Capt Sweet at first planned
for the Ordnance Team to start 1 October inspecting equipment turned
in by the Japanese Army.

Further investigation led to an inspection of the Kobe Steel
Works. The plant manager, who was interviewed and who acted as a
guide through the factory, "seemed very co-operative and answered all
questions that were asked".

The Kobe Steel Works had first been bombed 18 March 1945, but
little damage was sustained by the tank and tank gun sections of the
factory. It was bombed again on 5 June 1945 and severe damage was
wrought, although attempts were made to keep up the tank and gun
production. All work stopped on 5 July as the people would no longer
go to work for fear of being bombed. According to factory officials,
there was a shortage of steel, but labor problems kept the production
at low figure. The plant was government controlled, and even the
officials (apparently) were not well informed as to where or how the
gun and tanks were used.

Report on Himeji Cavalry School (Tanks)

The same Ordnance Team investigated the Himeji Cavalry Tank School
the proving ground at Himeji, (May, Incl 33) where three tanks were found
of a type different from any other recovered to that date. The tanks had
no means of being identified other than by a nameplate that did not give
complete information. All tanks were in fairly good condition, although
two showed signs of possible sabotage: the wires from the instrument
panel had been torn out from one, and a nameplate had been removed from
another.

It was thought that the tank might have been made by Mitsubishi
as the Kobe Steel Works were making the gun and shipping it to that
firm.

125

Arrangements were made with the 33rdDivision G-2 to pick up the responsible Japanese Officers and enlisted tank men of the school in order to obtain more information on the tank and to have experienced personnel to put the tanks in running condition. Photographs were taken and were submitted with the technical report.

Report on Ammunition for Kobe Anti-Aircraft Defenses

Capt Sweet's Ordnance Team also reported on the ammunition available for Kobe anti-aircraft defenses. All such ammunition was stored in a warehouse just north of pier 4, in Kobe. An inventory of the building disclosed the following:

```
436 rounds........ 12 c.m. bomb ammunition
874 rounds........  8 c.m. AA ammunition
2132 rounds........ 7 c.m. substitute
866 rounds........  7 c.m. blank
6736 rounds........ 7 c.m. AA ammunition
```

A 50-second mechanical time fuze was also discovered in the ammunition warehouse. It was thought that this fuze, manufactured in Tokyo in 1945, was a modified version of the type 91 fuze. The Osaka Air Station and the Kobe Fort Agency were investigated by this Ordnance personnel.

The Tokyo Electric Company

The Signal Team of Unit No. 51, composed of 1st Lt. James W. Elkins, T/Sgt Mario La Cognata, and T/3 Edmond E. Manna, investigated the Tokyo Electric Company, a subsidiary of General Electric of New York.

Before the outbreak of hostilities, the Kobe branch engaged in manufacture of commercial radio receivers, electric lamps and other electrical appliances. During the war, the plant was operated under strict government control and was allowed to make only Marine radio sets.

Approximately 150 people were employed at the factory. Of these, approximately 107 were Japanese school boys and the rest were adults employed in the office as clerks and typists.

The plant had not been in production since 5 June 1945, which was attributable to the fact that the water and electric supply to the Kobe area had been demolished, and because there was no longer a demand for Marine radio sets. The plant was about forty percent destroyed, with the receiver building completely demolished and facilities in the rest of the plant heavily damaged.

The Himeji Cavalry School and the 4th Replacement Unit of the Kobe Defense Division were also inspected by the Team.

Field Unit No.52

Field Unit No.52, the third Technical Intelligence Unit attached to I Corps, landed 25 September 1945 at Wakayama, Honshu, proceeded the following day to Osaka (May, Incl 33).

The Chemical Warfare Team, composed of 1st Lt Victor Del Guercio, Sgt Gordon F. Duckett, and Cpl Ralph C. Amouro, inspected the following targets: Nissho & Co., Ltd. This plant was a transportation agency for delivery of raw materials to manufacturers, and did not handle chemicals. Mitsubishi Co., Ltd., were dealers in food and other essential materials for civilians, and handled no chemicals.

Nippon Soda Company had its office in Osaka, its factories in Hokuriku District in Northwest Honshu. This company was a manufacturer of chemicals, but its plant was outside the Unit's area of operations. Yamada & Co. a wholesale house in chemicals, was destroyed by air raid. Miki & Co., Ltd., were wholesale dealers in phenol dyes. At the Naruo Naval Air Base some Chemical Warfare items were found, and some of these were new items. CWS equipment was also found at the Takeda Pharmaceutical Industries, Ltd. The Kitajima Powder Magazine Stored much ammunition, including some Chemical Warfare equipment. Chemical Warfare equipment was located at Tezukayama Girls High School, and much CWS ammunition was stored at the Uenoshiba Ammunition Plant.

New Chemical Warfare items which were recovered were: a gas-proof building containing t ree collective protectors; type 1, model 1, Signal smoke canle; type 3, model 1, Mark 27, 60 kg incendiary rocket bomb; no.1 incendiary candle; and a tear gas grenade.

1st Lt John E. Harms, T/4 Roger W. Sherwood, and Pvt B.G. Malamuth, Engineer Team for the Unit, inspected the following targets: Oki Denki K.K. demolished beyond recognition by fire bombs; Nippon Seitetsu KK. destroyed, a large supply of steel on hand in the yards ; Kubota Tekkosha KK. was in excellent condition, ready for peacetime production of 13-ton tractors and deisel engines. Osaka Seisa Zoki KK, located in the Nankai Building, Osaka City, manufactured machinery, weapons and ammunition; Sekiguchi Kikai Seisakusho KK, in Osaka City, had bout 90% of its area destroyed by fire bombs.

This team located near Sakai (Map, Incl 33) twenty-three carry all scrapers with a capacity of about eight cubic yards.

HISTORY OF TECHNICAL INTELLIGENCE

The Signal Team, 1st Lt Jack M. Daniels, M/Sgt Frederick J. Doll, and T/4 Robert R. Argal, Jr., investigated the following targets: Oki Denki K.K. was bombed to destruction and was of no Intelligence value; Nippon Denki Seiki KK was partially destroyed by bombing; Matsushita Denki Sangyo KK was intact and was at the time of investigation producing civilian radios; Sumitomo Kensha, Ltd., (same as above) had its buying office only in Osaka, which purchased materials for its plant in Tokyo. Osaka Imperial University was investigated for information referring to electronic research, but information secured was negligible. The Wireless Depot, located in Saegaji south of Sakai, was investigated; interrogation of the commanding officer of the 3rd Super Short Wave Company revealed that the Depot existed on paper only, but was equipped to furnish VHF radio-telephone link service between two telephone centrals - no equipment was received from this organization.

New items of equipment recovered by the Signal Team: VHF set used by anti-aircraft regiments; type 9? line construction, maintenance, and wire-laying vehicle that was full-tracked and specially built; type 18 air-ground liaison radio receiver; and a special super-short-wave radio receiver.

Capt Leslie F. Lawrence, S/Sgt Victor Bredehoeft, and T/4 Boyd M. Bierly, Field Unit No. 62 Ordnance Team, investigated Osaka Arsenal which produced all types of cannon above 37 mm. Approximately 80% of the producing shops in Osaka Arsenal had been destroyed on August 14 by bombs and approximately 50% of the machine tools had been damaged.

New weapons found by the term were: 12 cm AA dual purpose gun with director - this gun had overseas use only in Sumatra; 7 cm rocket gun (bazooka); 155 mm rocket gun (20 tubes) experimental model completed and tested, which was to have been produced by Osaka Arsenal; 155 mm rocket gun (6 tubes) which had not yet been tested - only two models had been produced; 75 mm AT gun to have been mounted on new tank - only three had been mounted on tanks - tanks were supposed to have been in Tokyo area.

All rifles in Osaka area had the serial number and manufacturer's mark ground off, possibly to conceal the total number, to conceal missing lots, or to conceal the manufacturer's identity, i.e., possibly German Mauser type.

Eighth Army Technical Intelligence Field Units

Assigned to Eight Army were the following Technical Intelligence units (personnel are included in operations roster, Incl 3).

Field Unit No. 4 ....XI Corps
Field Unit No. 53 ....XI Corps
Field Unit No. 5 ....XIV Corps
Field Unit No. 54 ....XIV Corps
Field Unit No. 55 ....IX Corps

Field Unit No. 4 and No. 53, both assigned to XI Corps in the
Tokyo area, cooperated closely with each other under the direction of
Major Jaroslav V. Klima, who also served as officer in charge of Ord-
nance with Unit No. 4.

They arrived in Yokohama (Map, Incl. 33) 12 September 1945, tracked
down assigned targets and during the course of this work encountered a
number of new installations. At the Tokyo Ordnance Supply Depot, Col
Matsumato supplied the units with a map showing the location of branch
depots under their control. When asked, he also informed them that
the name of the organization in charge of all Japanese Ordnance activities (in the Japanese Army this included Engineer, Chemical Warfare,
Signal and Ordnance) was the Army Ordnance Arsenal Administrative Headquarters, with Lt Gen Kan in charge. The equivalent to the U.S. Medical Corps was a separate agency with its headquarters at Yoga in Tokyo, while the equivalent to the U.S. Quartermaster Corps was small
enough so that it was run as a Staff Section of Imperial Headquarters.

The units established direct liaison with the Army Ordnance Administrative Headquarters through a Japanese staff officer of their Technical Department. From him the units received a list, in Japanese, of
all standard items of equipment, and a list of the Experimental Stations or Proving Grounds and their specialties in the XI Corps area.

Experimental Stations at Kokubunji

On 21 September a trip was arranged to the Experimental Station
at Kokubunji, (Map, Incl 33) inside whose walls there wer five of the
ten stations: Experimental Station #1 (machine guns, artillery, rocket
and ammunition research); Experimental Station #3 (Engineer equipment
research); Experimental Station #5 (Signal equipment research); Experimental Station #8(raw material research); and Experimental Station No.
2 (fire control and optical instruments), which had been moved to warehouses at Kokubunji from Kogenei when American troops occupied that
area. The complete installation at Kokubunji was also by this time
under rigid guard by American Division troops.

The trip to Kokubunji was arranged so that the heads of the various departments were present when the Technical Intelligence unit arrived. U.S. personnel attending were: Major Jaroslav V. Klima, officer
in charge of Unit #4; Capt Willard C. Holloway, officer in charge of
Unit #53; 1st Lt Alcide Santilli, Signal Corps officer of Unit #53;
and Ensign Gibson from NEIU (Navy).

After a general instruction, each officer separated from the group and investigated his specialty.

Station No.5 (Signal Corps) was visited by Lt Santilli.

Station No.5 (raw materials) was investigated by all personnel. The mission of this station was to investigate all types of raw materials for use by the Army, and it was recommended by Technical Intelligence officers present that if detailed information about processes were required, that qualified personnel be sent to interview the engineers available. Meanwhile, a preliminary interview was held with the chief officer of general affairs, and an officer from the organic chemistry department.

Station No.3 was visited by Maj Klima, Capt Holloway, and Ensign Gibson. Capt Holloway prepared a separate report on this Station.

Maj Klima and Ensign Gibson visited Station No.2, (fire control equipment and optics), originally located at Koganei. Many new items of fire control were observed and the warehouses were placed under guard until Technical Intelligence samples could be taken. Another officer was interviewed, but aside from some information about fungus growth on lenses and a few explanations of the Stations activities, little information could be obtained.

The last place examined was Experimental Station No.1 (machinery, guns, artillery, rockets, ammunition), where many Ordnance items of Technical Intelligence interest were found. Included were the following:

    15 cm AA gun (no type had been set)
    12 cm AA gun, type 3
    75 cm AA gun, type 4
    75 cm recoiless guns
    90 mm recoiless guns
    75 mm hand rocket launcher
    90 mm hand rocket launcher
    57 mm AT (anti-tank) guns
    75 mm AT gun (860 meter sec)
    75 mm AT gun (copy of German KWK, 75 mm tank gun)

The Major General and members of his staff were interviewed, and it was found that this station did the basic research and design on small arms, artillery, rockets and ammunition. The actual proof-firing was done at Futfsu (for small arms) and Ichi prefecture. In addition to specific data on various weapons, the following general information was obtained:

Some liaison was maintained with the Germans, but not the free exchange expected. For instance, the Japanese type 99, 88 mm AA gun, a direct copy of the FLAK 18 German 88, was copied from a gun captured in China and was not obtained from the Germans. The nozzle design on rockets was originally German, but was modified by the Japanese.

The Japanese received tube and recoil mechanisms for 75 mm KWK gun, PAK 38 50 mm AT gun, and PAK 40 75mm AT gun, plus the German PAK 41, 75/55 taper bore gun. When asked why they did not adopt them, they answered, "We had no mass production facilities."

The recoiless gun research was started by the Japanese when they heard of the Russian type, but was not pursued until the German one was seen in pictures and drawings.

In general, most equipment had been removed from the experimental stations at the time the T I units made their investigation, and was at that time under the control of Japanese Twelfth Army Headquarters. Through 1st Cavalry Division G-2 direct liaison was established with the various staff service officers of 12th Army to ascertain the location of all items of equipment of Technical Intelligence interest in the area. As a result, many items of new equipment were discovered, including 75 mm recoiless guns, 81 mm rocket launchers, models of new type tank guns, and Signal equipment. All Available standard items and development types of Japanese equipment in which the U. S. War Department was interested, were located and assembled; arrangements for this were completed at a separate meeting between the various officers of each service from the Technical Intelligence Units and from the Japanese Twelfth Army.

A trip was arranged with the Army Ordnance Administration Bureau for Ordnance, Signal, Chemical Warfare and IEU representatives to be escorted to Experimental Station #6 (CWS Research Laboratory) and Experimental Station #7 (Fundamental Physical Research Laboratory), both at Okuba. Much information of development, research and Technical Intelligence interest was uncovered.

In addition to the liaison already established, Lt Col Tait, at that time Chief of Central Liaison Section, G-2 GHQ (AFPAC), made the facilities of his section available if further contacts were required with any particular Japanese group.

Toward the end of September, Maj Klima attended a meeting at Anti-Aircraft Command F E F Headquarters to discuss the History of the 15 cm AA gun with the designers. Arrangements were made for the Japanese to turn over to him complete blue prints on this gun and on the 40 cm rocket which was at that time under development. He also received charts showing, in Japanese the characteristics of all standard propellant powders manufactured by the Japanese.

131

HISTORY OF TECHNICAL INTELLIGENCE

Other Installations Investigated

The Two Technical Intelligence untis with XI Corps collected large quantities of equipment at the following installations which they investigated:

Konishi Photography Co; manufactured aerial cameras photo chemicals prepared at Kanisawa, Nagano Prefecture.

Physics Department, University of Tokyo; no equipment of Intelligence interest recovered.

Jyuja Ordnance Warehouse: stored ammunition.

OJiku Akabane Army Clothing Warehouse: all Quartermaster supplies.

Itabashi Arsenal: small arms and ammunition.

Gas mask factory in Tokyo: reconverted to clothing manufacture.

Tokyo Arsenal No. 1: produced ammunition, fuzes, this was the installation later taken over as the TechnicalIntelligence Center.

Tokyo Arsenal No.2: construction material ammunition.

Oji Factory of Itabashi Factory, Tokyo Arsenal No.2: explosives.

Yokosuka Naval Arsenal

Army Chemical Warfare School (Narashino): important for CWS Intelligence.

Television Laboratory, Japan Broadcasting Company: director interviewed but little information secured.

Korakuen Stadium: on the main road in Urawa (Map, Incl 33), 30 AA guns with ammunition, searchlight, etc. recovered.

Tokyo Shibawa (formerly Matsuda): (Kanagawa, Kawasaki).

Tokyo Shibaura (Matsuda): radio tubes (Kanagawa, Kawasaki).

Sumitomo Communication Company (Tamagawa, Kanagawa).

Fuji Communication Company (Kanaski, Kanagawa).

Warehouses, Imperial Guard Grounds.

Hino Armored Car Co.: new type armored half-track manufacturing plant; not operating.

Tama Gun Powder Factory: extensive supplies of explosives; not operating.

Mayeda Heavy Machinery Co.: manufactured dudges, minesweeping floats, etc.; not operating.

Ito Paint and Lacquer Co.: not operating.

Tokyo Watanabe Seitai Co.: paper manufacturing.

Nippin Airplane Factory: air-frames and floats.

Tokyo Tanabe Pharmaceutical Co.: vitamin manufacturing.

Shimada Aluminum Company: airplane gas tanks.

Akamatsu Wool Co.: mohair.

Dai Nippin Bicycle Co.: in production.

Toakiki Machinery Co.: Navy 40 kg. FS smoke generators.

Tokyo Metal Refining Co.: scrap refining.

Tokushiboschin: bearing and brushing manufacturing.

Thuoko Gyo Co., Ltd.: type 94, 8mm pistols and 12.7mm type 1 aircraft machine guns, of which approximately 100 were in the assembly shop.

Sanyo Machinery Co.: turret lathes.

Tana Supply Office: comprised approximately 100 buildings; loading station for land mines and artillery ammunition.

Kanegafuchi Tractor Manufacturing Co.: 90 h.p. caterpillar tractors.

Plant in Soka: manufactured copper, brass, bronze alloys.

Storage area near Soka (Map, Incl 33): for bar steel, lumber, plaster, paint, lubricants, electrical supplies, automotive parts.

Narimasu Airfield: contained special purpose vehicles, explosives, clothing.

Great Japan Fertilizer Co: vitamins, condensed feed pills.

Tokyo Supply Dump #1, Warehouses #23, 43, 53: Signal and meteorological equipment; Unit No. 4 suggested a report on this installation be sent to IBF Weather Group to investigate.

Engineer Supply Depot, Chiba (Map, Incl 33); quantity of Engineer equipment as well as some Ordnance equipment; inventory was made by Japanese officials.

Chofu Air Strip: new items of clothing.

Koza Supply Dump: Ordnance items.

St. Luke's Hospital: taken over by 42nd General Hospital

Naval Medical College: trained Japanese Naval officers:

Tokyo Chanty Hospital: operated Naval Medical College.

Imperial Institute of Infectious Diseases.

Naval Hospital: inventory taken.

Showa Tsen Hospital: civilian.

Tokyo Army Medical Supply Hqs.: research conducted; papers translated.

Airfield: pyrotechnics.

Ichinomiya Gas Factory: gas bombs, blasting caps; large amounts of mustard gas produced; had gas protected equipment.

Sonoike Teel Co.: dyes, small tools.

Matsushita Dry Battery Co.: dry batteries - 4,000,000 in 1944.

Chigoski Radar Installations: Signal, Ordnance equipment.

Bagami Arsenal: new Ordnance equipment.

Futtsu Arsenal: equipment was thoroughly and systematically destroyed by the Japs; some new ammunition found.

Hiratsuka Naval Arsenal: found dark room and small quantities of printing paper and bulk ingredients for photo-chemicals; of much technical interest from powder analysis standpoint.

Kokabunji Proving Grounds: good supply of Signal equipment including some new developments; documents of this equipment.

Matsushita Dry Battery Co-Osaka Factory: producing flashlight batteries, but could produce quite a number of other types.

Sixth Military Laboratory, Okuba: gas bombs, projectiles; Chemical Warfare research.

Seventh Military Laboratory, Okuba: fundamental physical research; document on underwater barges for transporting munitions and fuel translated and forwarded to Naval authorities; information secured on 40mm rocket with built-in grange selector; summary of projects undertaken (translation by GHQ) secured.

Vitamin Factory: mostly burned; inoperative; few supplies secured.

Nippin Gun Powder Co., Ltd.: drugs for civilian use (reconverted).

Army Medical Supply Hq. at Yoga: obtained information on supplies; T.I. Unit suggested an investigation be made of a considerable quantity of silver bullion, gold, platinum, foil and wires in safe under (unarmed) Japanese guards.

Japanese Pioneer (Engineer) School at Matsudo (Map, Incl 33): considerable quantity of new Engineer equipment; all precision instruments and records disposed of before U.S. entry into Japan.

Showa-Fertilizer Co.: parent company of a syndicate consisting of the following:

> Kawasaki: Manufacturers of sulfate of ammonia, liquid ammonia, nitric acid.

> Kanose: lime-nitrogen, calcium carbide.

Okitsu: potassium chloride, potassium nitrate.

Tateyama: potassium chloride.

Hirota: potassium chlorate, sodium cyanide.

Shiojiri: artificial abrasives, fene-alloys.

Chichibu: fene-chrome.

Koum: pig iron.

Matsumoto: electralytic iron

Yokohama: alumina, graphite electrodes, caustic soda,
sulfuric acid.

Omachi: aluminum, artificial graphite.

Kitakata: aluminum

Toyama: alumina, aluminum.

All personnel of Field Unit No.4 screened equipment selected
from the above-listed targets and marked it as of Technical Intelligence interest. When the targets were first investigated no
decision as to warehouse space had been made (The Technical Intelligence Depot did not arrive until later), and none of the heavier
equipment was moved. At that time it was estimated that approximately
six 4-ton truck loads of small equipment plus various automotive equipment were ready for T.I. analysis.

Japanese Army Engineer School 1s Seized

Within a week after landing at Yokohama, and after much scrambling,
the two Engineer Teams of Field Units No. 4 and No. 53 and secured a
tent full of Engineer items. Then they obtained a lead from a Jap.
lieutenant general which led the teams to the Japanese Army Engineer
School (their Fort Belvoir), at Matsudo (Map, Incl 33) about fifteen
miles N. E. of Tokyo.

1st Lt Clinton O. Netter, T/3 James W. Ellyette, and T/3 Elsworth
P. Paris, Engineer Team of Unit No. 4, moved in and took the place
intact, complete with personnel and equipment. Arrangements were
made with the officer in charge for the Japanese to inventory the
equipment, and with the exception that no precision instruments,
blue prints, or office papers could be found (in one powder factory

a Japanese captain showed the team the pile of ashes where their records were burned), a large quantity of equipment was assembled at the School.

Using the facilities available at the School, Lt Potter and his team engaged in research of these items, and before the end of October submitted eleven reports on new equipment recovered. By that time all members of the team had moved into the 1st Cavalry Division and were awaiting orders for shipment to the United States for discharge from the Army.

Capt Millard C. Holloway, T/3 Charles W. Jenkins, and Pfc Philip Zarahn, members of Engineer Team No. 53, took over, and the two enlisted men hauled other Engineer items from Chiba into the School where all Engineer equipment was stored pending shipping instructions from the 5250th.

After the United States Army Technical Intelligence Depot arrived in Tokyo, Major Charles M. Hirst, Jr., officer in charge of the Engineer Analysis Section at the T.I. Center, and T/3 Jenkins, moved the equipment collected to the Tokyo Arsenal.

Cepharanthin, Drug Supposed To Cure Tuberculosis, Is Recovered

The Medical Team of Unit No. 4, 1st Lt John B. C. Muddiman and T/5 Norman N. Geron, reported an interrogation of Japanese medical personnel connected with the Tokyo Institute for Infections Diseases. This preliminary investigation was relative to cepharanthin, a Japanese-developed drug.

Special instructions issued to Lt Muddiman by the 5250th Technical Intelligence Company, dated 15 August 1945, read: "A drug called 'Cepharanthine' has been reported effective in this disease (tuberculosis). More specific information is needed on this subject".

The following articles were forwarded by air to the Medical Analysis Section, 5250th Technical Intelligence Company, by Lt. Muddiman

1. 10 grams crystalline alkaloids, total alkaloids from "Stephania Cepharantha", containing high percentage of cepharanthin

2. 1500 tablets, each containing 0.1 mg. "Cepharanthin"

3. 100 ampules, each containing 0.1 mg. "Cepharanthin", for injection.

4. 100 ampules, each containing 0.2.mg. "Cepharanthin" for injection

5. One volume, 924 pages, by Shuji Hassegawa, entitled, "Chemotherapy of Cepharanthin", in Japanese

6. One article, 2 pages, by Shuji Hassegawa, entitled "Experimental and Clinical Studies on Cepharanthin against Tuberculosis, Leprosy , and whooping Cough", in German.

7. One article, 13 pages, reporting favorable results in use of cepharanthin against pulmonary tuberculosis, in Japanese

8. One article, 3 pages, reporting favorable results in the use of Cepharanthin against whooping cough, in Japanese.

9. One article, 3 pages, reporting favorable results in the use of cepharanthin against asthma, in Japanese.

Lt Muddiman and T/5 Beron interviewed a professor at the Imperial Institute of Infectious Disease, Tokyo, and the director of the Fundamental Institute for Chemotherapy, Ichikawa, Pioneer in the research on the drug; a surgeon-captain, tuberculosis consultant for the Japanese Naval Medical College, Tokyo; and approximately ten Japanese civilian physicians in high positions. Among these, opinion was sharply divided, some believing the drug "useless".

Lt Muddiman reported, "If Cepharanthin has the properties some claim for it, it is of great importance. However, field analysis is completely impractical and no attempt is made herein to estimate its merit."

The president of the Naval Medical College, Tokyo, and his tuberculosis consultant were interviewed by the Medical Team of Unit No.4 at the Naval Medical College, Tokyo.

Medical Technical Intelligence Team No.4 also reported on the "Standard Procedure in the Japanese Navy for Treatment of Gonorrhea and Syphilis". This information was obtained from Japanese Navy Medical officers.

Large Quantities of Medical Equipment Recovered

Japanese equipment recovered by the team is listed below. None of these items had been previously reported by Medical Technical

Intelligence, and all items were in serviceable condition. An additional quantity of new equipment -- about the same number of items -- was also taken by the team, but had not yet been inventoried at the time of their report:

Water testing kit
Field laboratory, complete
Field X-ray plant, complete
Gas and water testing laboratory
Portable field hospital
Water filter in chest
Gas casualty chest
Hypodermic chest
Microscopic accessories chest
Field sterilizer chest
Folding dental chair, in chest
Ozone generator
Electrometer, in chest
Air-drop water container
Parachute for above
Lung capacity meter
Gas analyzer
Air-drop parachute (supplies)
Fluoroscope for use with 35 mm camera
Bamboo litter
Arm strength tester, in case
Blood pressure kit
Indirect blood transfusion set
Dispensing kit, wood
Reservoir for stomach pump
Ear and nose kit, with case
Polygraph, with case
Eye chart case
Stereoptican glasses, case
Hydrometer set
Microscope, folding, medium, leitz
Microscope, folding, medium, new type
Microscope, type undetermined
2 cameras, 35mm, in case, for use with fluoroscope, Army
2 cameras, 35mm, in case, for use with fluoroscope, Navy
Over 100 new drugs and medicines
Assorted medical chemicals
Assorted scientific papers

The entire period of the latter half of October was spent by members of both Units No. 4 and No. 53 in evacuating, arranging to be evacuated, and consolidating selected items of Japanese equipment of Technical Intelligence value. These were collected in various central locations for close control and more effective guarding to help prevent premature (officially ordered) destruction. These places were: the Chemical Warfare School at Narashimo, where equipment was being prepared for shipment by the Eighth Army Chemical office; the Engineer School at Matsudo, where equipment was being moved to the Technical Intelligence Center Depot, recently established; the Technical Intelligence warehouse at 1st Cavalry Division C.P. area; Tokyo Supply Depot; Akabane Ammunition Depot.

By the end of October the following officers and enlisted men from the two field units, 4 and 53, had been made available on the point system and had either left or were about to depart for the United States:

Field Unit No. 4

Capt George I. Ford, SC
Capt Kenneth H. Bowman, QMC
1st Lt Clinton O. Potter, CE
T/Sgt Louis J. Magagna, CWS
T/3 Elsworth P. Paris CE
T/3 James W. Ellyett, CE
T/5 Frank E. Brown, Jr., CWS
Pfc Juan O. Gonzales, QMC

Field Unit No. 53

Capt Willard C. Holloway, CE
1st Lt Nicholas Townsan, Ord
1st Lt Francis K. Switzer, CWS
S/Sgt Kurt M. Richter, SC
Pfc Philip Zarahn, CE

Field Units No. 54 and No. 5 with XIV Corps

Technical Intelligence Field Units No. 54 and No.5 were on temporary duty to XIV Corps Headquarters, which landed at Shiogama, Honshu (Map, Incl 33), 16 and 17 September 1945. Headquarters moved on the 17th to Sendai, Honshu (Map, Incl 33), and both units operated out of that area in the ensuing months.

2d Lt Robert A. Pontius, Sgt William N. Davidson, Pfc Carl C. Cureton, CWS Team No. 54, investigated the Army and Navy Arsenals at

Sendai, but found no new CWS equipment. The Navy Arsenal had an acid plant and small testing laboratory, both of which had been dismantled and the majority of the equipment removed. Both Arsenals appeared to have been used as a division of the main Ordnance Arsenal rather than for Chemical Warfare purposes.

2d Lt Frank G. Pospisil, S/Sgt Richard T. Smith, and Pfc Frank M. Ledesma, Engineer Team for Unit No. 54, investigated both Army and Navy Arsenals at Shirana, but found no equipment.

Ordnance Team No. 54, 1st Lt Henry L. Abbott, T/4 Gerald C. Lockridge, Pfc Charles R. Kabele, when they inspected the Tayajo Navy Arsenal at Shiogama, found the production was 20mm shells, type 99 20mm aircraft cannon, type 38 aircraft flexible 7.7mm machine guns, incendiary bombs and parachute flares. Most of the machinery for the plant had been moved underground.

Upon inspection of the Sendai Branch of Tokyo Arsenal, they found most of the plant disassembled. Production had been 20mm ammunition and fuzes, with powder shipped in from other sources. A few boxes of ammunition were on hand, including several hundred rounds of type 90 88mm and type 100 fuzes for these shells. The teams also found four type 2 Army AA Correctors (directors), different from the type 2 Navy AA directors previously recovered. These that were found were in good condition, with two new ones packed for shipment, and the other two stripped of the meters.

At an unused airfield one mile east of Sendai, Ordnance Team No. 54 recovered 18 type 99, 88m dual purpose, pedestal mount, antiaircraft guns, manufactured in early 1945. It was believed that several of these were reported in the Southern Philippine Islands campaign, but they had been destroyed. At the same airfield they also took approximately 300 rounds of type 100, 88mm ammunition and approximately 300 fuzes type 100, mechanical time, AA.

The last few days in October this same team inspected stock piles of collected Japanese Ordnance to determine if there were any equipment of Intelligence value at the following points: Yamagata, Yonezawa, Sakata, Akita, and Morioka (Map, Incl 33). The following items of Intelligence value were found:

> 3 - Ho 401, 57mm aircraft cannon. This item was stored at 11th Airborne Division Artillery, Akita, under the control of the S-4 until disposition was given by the 5250th, due to arrive in Japan shortly.

                1 - type 30, caliber 6.5mm rifle
                1 - type 30, caliber 6.5mm Carbine
                1 - 22 year type, caliber 7.7mm rifle

By that time, the end of October, Akita Prefecture had completed the collection of all Japanese equipment, and the destruction of ammunition: Iwate Prefecture had completed the collection of all Japanese equipment, and by 10 November had all ammunition dumped at sea: Yamagata Prefecture had all Japanese equipment collected in three cities and disposition had been started on ammunition.

The Signal Team, 2nd Lt Leslie R. Mellichamp, Jr., S/Sgt Lloyd K. Hughes, S/Sgt Robert A. Rictor, also investigated the Naval Arsenal at Shiogama and the Army Arsenal at Sendai, but found no Signal equipment. Upon checking the government-owned radio station, JXQ, Sendai, they found equipment of commercial manufacture, but no new developments were noted.

Equipment was found and reports were submitted on the Japan Electric Co., Sendai: the Airforce radio station near Jimmachi; a radio installation on the island of Kinkazan; and the Naval fixed station TEMIHE, near Ono.

Technical Intelligence Unit No. 5

Technical Intelligence Unit No. 5 also landed with Headquarters XIV Corps and moved on to Sendai. Shortly after they arrived Capt Beryl L. Light, officer in charge of the Unit, returned to the United States on the point system and 1st Lt Jerry L. White took over. The two enlisted men, S/Sgt Glenn L. Haugen and T/4 William J. Sauer, the balance of the Signal Team that Capt Light had headed, were then transferred for temporary duty to the 11th Airborne Division, XIV Corps, where they were ordered to assist in collecting and destroying Japanese equipment.

The Engineer Team (Lt Jerry L. White, T/4 Eugene W. Fields, Pfc Henry Carson) were used by the XIV Corps Engineer Section to look for and make reports on the location of Engineer construction materials. Investigation of a pontoon bridge dump at Maiyachi, Honshu, revealed that materials were used for an Engineer School and were in poor condition. Investigation of the dump of Tohoku 129th Corps, Sendai, was made, but materials had been used for training purposes, and no new items were discovered. By November, Pfc Carson had been relieved of assignment with the team.

HISTORY OF TECHNICAL INTELLIGENCE

The CWS Team (2d Lt John A. Wagner, Sgt Levere D. Brown, Pvt Willie Wimberly) recovered equipment in the 122d Infantry Unit and the 2d Cavalry Regiment bivouac areas, and submitted reports on their findings. Investigations of other units in the Sendai area, however, resulted in no new findings

After acting as disposition teams with 11th Airborne Division in the middle of October, the team investigated the Ichinomiya Naval Arsenal and recovered items of Technical Intelligence value from this arsenal and from Shimoshizu Chiba Airfield. These included:

    4 Navy experimental type #3 chlorine gas masks
          (16th year model)
    8 portable gas chamber tents
    3 flame thrower tanks, 5-gun model
    3 gas sprayers (tracked trailer)

By 10 November all members of this team had been relieved of temporary duty to return to their proper station.

Targets investigated by the Medical Team, 1st Lt Harold M. Jones and Pfc Clifford E. Harrelson, included: Japanese 2d Cavalry Regiment bivouac area in Sendai, the Sendai Branch Depot (Medical) at Nanakita, Sendai Army Hospital #2 at Matsuda (Miyagi-ken), and the Yamagata Army Hospital at Yamagata.

Ordnance equipment of Intelligence interest was identified and segregated by the Ordnance Team (1st Lt Kenneth L. Warden, Jr., T/5 John R. Smallwood, Pfc Andrew Nadas) working in conjunction with the 357th Ord Depot Co. at the following installations: Sendai Army Arsenal, Naval Arsenal at Shiogama and Matsushima, Shirasawa Ammunition Dump, Yamagata Electrochemical Co. and the area of the 105th Regiment at Fukushima (Map Incl 33). New items recovered:

          12.7mm high explosive round for Browning type gun
          20mm H. E. round for Ho 5 cannon
          20mm practice round for type 98 and 99 guns
          type 98 fuze for instantaneous or short delay action
          70mm rocket launcher
          light personnel carrier accommodating eight persons

HISTORY OF TECHNICAL INTELLIGENCE

Unit No. 55 with IX Corps

Technical Intelligence Unit No. 55 was placed on temporary duty with Headquarters, IX Corps. During September the Ordnance Team (1st Lt Charles E. Sloop, Pfc Donald W. Linstedt, Pfc William H. Kennedy) was attached to the 81st Division, and landed with them, 25 September, on Green Beach, Ao ori, Honshu (Map Incl 33). On 26 September they reported to the 322nd Infantry Regiment in Hirosaki (Map Incl 33), where they investigated two armories and the District Division Ordnance Depot, but no new equipment was located. 29 September they reported to the 323rd Infantry Regiment where they investigated the Japan Iron Sand Ino Co. and other known storage places of arms. They also reported to the 321st Regiment to inspect ammunition of which disposition was being made.

Early in October another Ordnance Team of Unit No. 55 (Capt Walter E. Swain, Pfc Ben T. Garcia, Pfc Morton H. Rosen) was placed on temporary duty to the Chief Ordnance Officer, IX Corps. After arrival at Sapporo, Hokkaido (Map Incl 33), this team operated in the Asari area where an ordnance dump, encountered by the 77th Infantry Division, was reported to the team for inspection. The installation was primarily an ammunition dump, and the small amount of Ordnance equipment stored there was classified as standard.

The CWS Team (1st Lt John M. Kapp, T/4 John L. Mooney, Cpl Buster Bentley) enroute to Hokkaido aboard the USS La Porte, sent a wire to 77th Division to guard Nippon Soda Co., manufacturers of war gasses, which was listed in the target folder as at Hakodate (Map, Incl 33). This company was a number one priority rating according to War Department research.

The team landed and set up at Sapporo, Hokkaido with Headquarters IX Corps, 6 October 1945. Previous investigation by the Division Artillery Headquarters indicated that the Nippon Soda Co. was not in Hokkaido, but in Honshu. A recheck by members of the T. I. team resulted in the following:

Lt Kapp contacted a Methodist minister who told him that a professor at Hakodate College would be an authority on chemical plants of military significance. This professor obliged them by guiding the team to the following plants:

144

Nissan Chemical Industrial Co., Ltd., Hakodate,
    manufacturers of sulphuric acid
Koatsu Kogyo Co., manufacturers of Oxygen and
    calcium super phosphate
Toyokoatsy Chemical Co. at Sunogawa, manufacturers
    of ammonia sulphate and ammonia gas
Konetsukogyo Co. at Asonocho, manufacturers of oxygen
    and acetyline from calcium carbinde

But none of the above plants manufactured war gases.

Further search and interrogation verified the previous report
that the Nippon Soda Company was not, as indicated in the War Department target folder, in Hakodate, but that it was in Honshu.

Investigation of all other targets listed in the folder, and
many more discovered independently by the team, resulted in the
recovery of considerable quantities of Chemical Warfare materiel.

The Engineer Team (2d Robert E. Vannice, T/5 David L. Barker,
Pfc James H. Riggs) reported that the lack of Engineer equipment
on Hokkaido, with the exception of building materials and the equipment for handling them was notable. The unit also assisted in investigating certain industrial plants for the purpose of rehabili-
tation.

Awards received by T. I. Men of 5250th

Awards given to men who served with the 5250th Technical Intelligence Company in the Pacific Theater are shown in Inclosure 34.

And Now...

7 December 1945, Tokyo, Japan. The war is over and many in
the Army, including men from the 5250th, are going home -- and
hoping to reach there by Christmas.

In peace time, Intelligence, and especially that parvenue,
Technical Intelligence, slips into bad repute -- not only with
the ordinary American Citizen who considers it a menace to U. S.
peace-intentioned international diplomacy, but what is much more
to the point, with the United States Army itself, which has had
a tendency to consider that in peace time Intelligence is...super-
fluous. If we are not to be the blind leading the blind, there
should be a change in that policy.

HISTORY OF TECHNICAL INTELLIGENCE

Technical superiority available to a nation will be the most determinate factor, next time, in deciding who is to win, who is to lose. There is only one means of finding out the technical innovations of other nations — that is by an efficiently staffed, effectively operating Technical Intelligence Department. Next time we must be one jump ahead, not one jump behind.

www.ingramcontent.com/pod-product-compliance
Lightning Source LLC
Chambersburg PA
CBHW080510110426
42742CB00017B/3062